TOULOUSE-LAUTREC

Court Painter to the Wicked

THE LIFE AND WORK OF
TOULOUSE-LAUTREC

BY

JEAN BOURET

HARRY N. ABRAMS, INC. · PUBLISHERS · NEW YORK

TRANSLATED FROM THE FRENCH
BY DAPHNE WOODWARD

CONTENTS

FOR MADAME JEAN WALTER IN ADMIRATION

FOREWORD

In the Introduction to his *La Vie et l'œuvre de Valéry Larbaud*, which
sets an unparalleled standard for the biography of a writer, G. Jean
Aubry declares: 'All I have done here is to tell the story of a literary
life, dwelling on such facts as may have helped to mould the writer
and his works. All artistic creation is to some extent affected by
circumstances, and the historian should assemble these and shed the
clearest light he can on them, attempting only to indicate, not to
interpret, the mysterious role of talent or genius. The particular
conditions of his birth, temperament, period, connections and friend-
ships, cannot explain everything about a man's career, much less an
artist's: even the most determined character is at the mercy of un-
accountable impulses. But one can at least try to define the part played
by these.' The life of Larbaud which follows should be a model for
every study of the kind; but only the constant associate of a creative
artist can trace the development of his work from day to day, as is
done there.

In writing of a great man of the past, we can only rely on what are
known as 'the records', and hope that contemporary witnesses will

HORSEWOMAN FOLLOWED BY GROOM, 1880
Museum of Albi

prove to have been clear-sighted and sincere. Unfortunately, legend and history are more often based on a shaky, if glamorous, foundation of lies.

What is left of a man after he has been squeezed between the covers of a biography—the literary equivalent of the culinary 'liquidizer' that separates the juice from the pulp? We are left either with a faded, touched-up portrait, like an old photograph found at the back of a drawer, a dessicated shape, as colourless and brittle as a pressed flower from some album of our childhood, or else with a crude 'tuppence-coloured' print where the blue has run into the red and the engraver's tool has transformed his subject for all eternity—the snub nose into a Greek profile, the blackguard into a dashing cavalier, or the weak man into a saint.

Evidence is too often a counterfeit coinage: Saint-Simon, for all his determination to be impartial, is not always truthful. And what about Bachaumont, with his *Mémoires Secrets pour servir à l'histoire de la*

TWO HORSES WITH ORDERLY, 1880
Museum of Albi

République des Lettres which we take for gospel and are continually quoting? He was likeable, enquiring, intelligent, full of taste, tolerance and wit, but his journal is a mixture of truth and lies, salt and pepper, a mixture familiar to us ever since Plutarch, who was such a favourite with the usually discerning Montaigne.

Yet the art of biography has steadily grown in stature, even overshadowing the novel at certain periods. What are Maurois's novels, compared with his biographies of Byron, Disraeli, Shelley and the other figures he has chosen? And Mauriac the novelist surely takes second place to Mauriac the author of that little masterpiece, his *Vie de Jean Racine*, with its ringing echoes of pain?

Everything we know about the Italian painters has come to us through that gossip, Giorgio Vasari; and his anecdote about Titian's brush is as vivid as though we had witnessed the scene ourselves, though it teaches us nothing about Titian as an artist. We like to hear everything about a painter, and though the art historian is well aware that even the most carefully written biography can teach us little about its subject's actual work, we read it just as closely, for there is magic in other people's lives.

Broadly speaking, biography is a thing of our own time. The twentieth century is the age of 'lives', some romanticized, some strictly factual. The books about painters are so many that a choice would be invidious. An exception should be made, however, for Perruchot, a pioneer in the field, who specialized in biography which was well documented without being dull, poetical without sacrificing truth — yet different from such monumental works as that of Escholier on Delacroix, published some years before the war, which stands as a milestone of biographical progress.

But now to take a specific instance, that of Henri de Toulouse-Lautrec. It is little more than sixty years since Lautrec died; some of his friends, such as Francis Jourdain, lived on into our own day. We can obtain first-hand documents about him — photographs, press cuttings, letters; there has not been time for his pictures to get lost. And yet we are compelled to check and re-check all this information. We can trace

LE BOSC, ARTILLERY, 1879
Museum of Albi

his complicated list of addresses, discover the names of his associates and models, and put dates to his various paintings. But what of his private life? He came of an ancient family, full of taboos, and it systematically confused the trail. His mother took the initiative in this, while his father and his uncle burnt pictures, tore up letters. Did someone suggest Lautrec was an alcoholic? A prudish denial was the family rejoinder. Incidents of his life were concealed by some of his friends, Maurice Joyant for instance, and imagination, the mother of error, then set to work. It becomes hard to distinguish truth from fiction. Even confidences are untrustworthy. A woman who slept with the painter denies it a fortnight later, and Lautrec himself boasts of some things he has not really done. Whom are we to believe? Mauriac writes in his life of Racine: 'Every destiny is individual, unique, but when an author decides to write the biography of one man among a thousand others, it is because he feels attuned to his chosen master. The best way of approach to a man of the past is through one's own self.' If that is so, Lautrec raises a curious problem. One may well feel attuned to his outlook on life, to his sovereign contempt for the extraneous, his sharp judgments, his mocking humour; but to follow them up through one's own self is a different matter, for Lautrec's mental make-up is exceptionally subtle. It is, in fact, that of a cripple—notwithstanding his determination, which was only increased by difficulties.

What thus remains in common is taste, and the search for truth. We cannot enter Lautrec's world unless we accept the unvarnished evidence of our eyes, unless our predilection in painting is for the acutely perceived rather than for the imaginative, the surrealistic, the soft and smooth.

One more point—the last but not the least, and there is a catch in it. Much has already been written about Lautrec, and this is not the first biography of him. He has already been 'placed' by Joyant, Coquiot, Jourdain, MacOrlan, Adhémar, Lassaigne, Julien, Perruchot, to mention no others. All that remained for the biographer was to try to arrive at a closer view of him, in his own day, surrounded by the slightly unsavoury life of the Paris he knew; to show him as an artist with a multitude of problems, and to describe how he solved them.

Beyond a man's life there is his influence. Lautrec's, we must admit, has been slight compared with Cézanne's, for instance. But the present day seems particularly propitious for the triumph of his harsh art.

COUNT CHARLES DE TOULOUSE-LAUTREC, THE ARTIST'S UNCLE, 1882
Museum of Albi

CÉLEYRAN: OLD MAN, 1882
Museum of Albi

AT THE SOURCE OF THE RIVER

'The first thought of the biographer who wishes to advance his knowledge of a man is to turn to his ancestors. Even the most singular individual is only the fleeting expression of a race. What one needs is to trace the river back to its countless sources, in order to capture the secret of all the contradictions, all the eddies that make up a single being.'

FRANÇOIS MAURIAC, *Vie de Jean Racine*

On 9th September 1901, a man lay dying in a room behind closed shutters, through which a ray of sunlight forced its way as far as his bed. Flies buzzed in a thundery atmosphere that made them even more exasperating than usual. The man drew in a last breath of air, peered at the unfinished picture he had started early that summer, muttered something inaudible—legend has it that catching sight of his father, who was trying to drive away a fly, he remarked: '*Vieux c . . .*'—stiffened beneath the sheet he had seized in a feverish hand as though trying to reduce its weight, and fell back, defeated. Henri Marie Raymond de Toulouse-Lautrec Monfa, the last Count of Toulouse of his line, died thus at the Château de Malromé.

He was thirty-seven years old, and left behind him, scattered through a variety of studios, galleries and brothels, pictures as admirable as ever a painter planned or achieved. He was destined for

OLD WOMAN SEATED ON A BENCH AT CÉLEYRAN, 1882
Museum of Albi

resounding posthumous fame, and his right to it has never been contested. In himself he was an embodiment of history.

For long ages, history and legend have been interwoven. A blind poet cast a glow over Greece that has never faded. Grandmothers spun stories for their grandchildren about certain kings of France until they came to believe that those kings had created France. Not until much later did people realize that it was not, after all, 'forty kings who created France in a thousand years', as the *Action Française* declared, but that it was scarcely forty families, often at odds with the King and with fate, who had somehow managed to implant civilization on the territory they divided between them. And one of the families, which secured one of the finest positions, was that of the Counts of Toulouse, who held sway over Languedoc, from the Atlantic to the Mediterranean and from the Pyrenees to the mountains of Central France, until the fourteenth century.

Henri de Toulouse-Lautrec, who died on that 9th September like a stream vanishing in the sands, was the last of the river with its 'countless sources'. His death, like that of many of his ancestors, was both illogical and tragic; it did not crown his work, but broke it off and left it in suspense. Such were the deaths of the Crusaders: of Count Raymond IV, who led his southern knights to the Holy Land and was killed there in 1105, of Count Bertrand, of Count Alphonse of Toulouse, who was baptized in the Jordan—all of them descended from the first Count whom Charlemagne, when he was crowned at Rheims, had recognized as an independent vassal, granting him the privilege of wearing spurs on that occasion.

The importance of the Counts of Toulouse was not merely political and military, it was essentially of a moral and intellectual character. In those feudal days it was only through force of personality that an overlord could win acceptance from his men. Because the Counts of Toulouse had the prestige of great military leaders and because they were cultivated lovers of the beautiful, they were able to enlarge their estates and even had hopes of uniting them into a kingdom.

For five hundred years they added to their acres. Raymond IV, set on the Crusades, neglected his lands; but Raymond V married Con-

CÉLEYRAN: AN AVENUE, 1882
Museum of Albi

stance, daughter of Louis VI, and seems to have stepped into France of the Capet period booted, helmed, with treasure across his saddle.

During this epoch Toulouse became a capital city as brilliant as Paris, full of splendid buildings. But it was not entirely concentrated at one point: the Abbey of Saint-Guillaume du Désert and the Château de Cordes arose before the great arches of Saint-Étienne de Toulouse—the first upthrust of Gothic architecture, just as the poems in praise of Adélaïde de Toulouse, Viscountess of Carcassonne and Dame de Burlats, were the first French lyrical ballads.

Raymond VI, who married Joan of England, daughter of Henry II and Eleanor of Aquitaine and sister of Richard Cœur-de-Lion, was the first adventurer in the Toulouse family. In 1207 he was excommunicated by Pope Innocent III, who accused him of being a cheat, a lecher, and indulgent to heretics. He thereupon joined the twenty thousand and their 'rabble' who were then making their way down the Rhone Valley to attack the heretical Albigenses. After fighting against Simon de Montfort, he pretended to take his part in order to save his town; but too much blood had been shed already. The lives of the sixty thousand men whose throats had been cut by the followers of Almaria, the Papal Legate, to the cry of 'God will recognize His own', weighed heavily in the balance. Raymond VI captured Beaudoin, his brother, and hanged him. When he himself died the bloodshed was still continuing. Raymond VII succeeded in recapturing Toulouse from the Christian armies, but his subjects were weary; his only daughter married the brother of Louis IX of France (St Louis) and in 1271 the estates reverted to the French crown.

COUNT DE TOULOUSE-LAUTREC DRIVING THE MAIL-COACH TO NICE, 1881
Musée du Petite Palais, Paris

Toulouse as the single name of a family was heard no more; a tangled skein of genealogies must be unravelled to recover its traces. In 1169, eighteen years before his death, Beaudoin, the head of the younger branch, married Alix, Viscountess de Lautrec, the last descendant of a noble house of the Tarn region, and the two names were linked thereafter—sometimes with a third, Monfa, that of another allied family. Names were collected now as lands had been in an earlier age. Not that this indicated any fading of the colourful personalities of the Counts of Toulouse. Three Marshals of France were to be born of their mixed blood, contributed by kings' mistresses, impoverished country nobility, captains and adventurers. But persistent intermarriage soon began to weaken the strain. Raymond IV, already, had been excommunicated for marrying his first cousin, and the need to keep hold of the possessions and lands was a frequent cause of turmoil. The Toulouse-Lautrecs, even their women, were quarrelsome and sensual; the chroniclers describe with equal objectivity the courage of Odet de Foix, Viscount de Lautrec, killed at the siege of Naples in 1527 after narrowly escaping death at Ravenna, the debauchery of Pierre Joseph de Toulouse-Lautrec and the amorous excesses of Adélaïde de Toulouse, 'A qui dans la journée il en fallait douze'—but whose eclecticism might be interpreted as a form of democracy.

Quarrelsome and sensual, but also sensitive to a certain kind of nobility of character, and passionately attached to their native soil, the Toulouse-Lautrecs were aware of their strongholds, fields and vineyards as tangible realities, and they stopped at nothing to keep them and to acquire more. In 1863 there was an intermarriage between Count Alphonse de Toulouse-Lautrec Monfa and his cousin, Adèle Zoé Tapié de Céleyran. Her title was not so ancient as that of Lautrec, for it was only in 1798 that Esprit Jean-Jacques Toussaint Tapié was adopted by his cousin, Jacques Mengau, Seigneur of Céleyran and Councillor of the Audit Office at Montpellier, from whom he inherited his title and lands. But the Tapiés came of respectable bourgeois stock, had served the Crown as judges, councillors, treasurers, and even produced several very erudite Churchmen. Their wealth had steadily increased, as they accumulated plots of land and town houses,

COUNTESS ADÈLE DE TOULOUSE-LAUTREC IN THE SALON AT MALROMÉ, 1887
Museum of Albi

country mansions and vineyards. At the time of the cousins' marriage, the Céleyran estate alone comprised some two thousand five hundred acres of vines. By all the laws of genetics, this influx of bourgeois virtues should have done something to cool the fiery Lautrec blood; but Adèle—gentle and tactful—was perhaps not the woman to steady Count Alphonse.

Alphonse was the son of the 'Black Prince', a notable eccentric and mighty hunter. His father was killed when out with the harriers on Christmas Day 1871, and Alphonse was to meet the same death: flung from his horse down the steep, rocky side of the Viaur valley, near the Château du Bosc. Legend says that beside his body was found the hunting-horn which, as he lay bleeding, he had blown until his last breath, calling for help like Roland at Roncevaux.

With his handsome features, black hair and massive frame—like the oaks of the Tarn, broader than they are tall—Count Alphonse de Toulouse-Lautrec cut a considerable figure in local society. He had not inherited the insolent arrogance of his forbears, but pride in his name and birth led him to regard his fellow provincials as people of no account. He was often polite to them when he met them, but he seldom did meet them, and in life he followed only his own vagaries, which were considerable. After passing through Saint-Cyr he had been posted to the garrison at Maubeuge as a sub-lieutenant in the Sixth Lancers. He took advantage of this military period to perfect his horsemanship, and became the pride of his Regiment. Back at Albi, he did not know what to do with his leisure. Politics was suggested but he refused to entertain the idea, for he had an equal dislike for the Second Empire, the Republicans and the Orléanists. He was hostile to power in all its manifestations—a dandy and an anarchist who respected nothing and was at liberty to be so, being rich and having no-one to question his attitude. Perhaps he bore a secret grudge against his wife because marriage had obliged him to leave the army; for a young, good-looking and wealthy officer, garrison life, with its racemeetings, dinner-parties and brief love-affairs, must have been far from disagreeable. He never mentioned it, treated his wife with polished, aristocratic courtesy, but ignored all her appeals for sensible behaviour.

What he liked best was to astonish people. This led him to set up a Kirgiz tent in the Place de la Cathédrale at Albi, close to his own residence, the ancient Hôtel du Bosc, and go out to sleep there at night; to wash his linen in the gutter of the Place de la Madeleine when on a visit to Paris; to milk his mare in the Bois de Boulogne and then drink the milk before the round eyes of the assembled crowd; to dress up as a highlander with a kilt, as a Circassian, as a Crusader or as a cowboy. The East had attracted his ancestors, and Persian civilization fascinated him; he collected books on the subject, wrote out Persian cookery recipes for his friends, and studied the Persian methods of training a hawk, harnessing a horse, and riding. His gifts would have made him a remarkable ethnologist—as shown, for instance, in a drawing he did for his mother of the Caucasian helmet he wore when out in the Bois. It is a rapid but very detailed sketch. But he was not interested in any settled occupation.

He enjoyed travelling about France from one hunting party to another, at the whim of friendship and invitations. He is said—the anecdote is related by Perruchot—to have forgotten his wife on a station platform; for his passion for hunting was stronger than his love of home life, and Adèle was not physically congenial to him. She was sweet, dreamy, languid; he preferred the inn servants, shepherd-esses and middle-class women of easy virtue with whom he could make love in some barn before riding off again in pursuit of stag or hare, with his spirit and senses appeased. The break came in 1868. Henri their first-born child, was then four years old, and his brother, Richard had died on 27th August of that year at their country house at Loury, in Sologne. There was no divorce for the discomfited wife, only a complete estrangement, after which young Adèle's one idea was to bring up her son—now her only child—as a man after her own heart. Before we embark upon the story of Lautrec's life, here is a masterly passage from Thadée Natanson, to offset the foregoing list of ances-tors: 'Lautrec might have boasted—had he been capable of such a thing—that he was the lineal descendant of King Louis the Fat. His ancestors fought in many climes. He himself was the last bud of the tree, filled to bursting-point with sap that had long been gorged with

COUNT ALPHONSE DE TOULOUSE-LAUTREC, THE ARTIST'S FATHER, 1881
Museum of Albi

COUNTESS ADÈLE DE TOULOUSE-LAUTREC, THE ARTIST'S MOTHER, 1885
Museum of Albi

blood, heated with violence and cruelty; for his race had indulged too freely in pleasure and sought it in its uttermost refinements. To the family tree he added a fruitless branch, but it bore the rarest flowers. It may be that no Count de Toulouse or Viscount de Lautrec would have been able to understand the strange victories of this great-great-nephew. Yet there is every prospect that his fame will outlive theirs.

'Each man we set eyes on has exactly the same number of ancestors. But in the immense majority of cases these have bequeathed, apart from the multifarious flora of their instincts, merely a heritage of servitude. It is only from those who were for a long time wealthy or often bold, that a man's blood and nerves can retain some rather individual bequests. Lautrec was of strong stock. When he let himself go, he became terrifying. Lautrec could have been born in a slum and have been just the same. It is possible that many of his qualities of mind were inherited from his long line of ancestors. But at least he had the air of having bestowed them upon himself. He never used his title because he took too much pride in the one he had set himself to win.'

CHILDHOOD

'One so rich in laurels can well spare a rose
ROBESPIERRE

The silence of Albi, and its changing light. Beneath a sky that often dazzles, the ancient capital of the Catharans has a Florentine grace. Sainte-Cécile glows with the rosy tint of its age-old bricks. From the terraces of the palais de la Berbie, which so much resembles the Bargello, we look out over a great prospect of rolling hills, some green, some burnt brown. Below, in the foreground, flows the Tarn, making its pebbly way between houses, vineyards and gardens. Is it really the Tarn, or the Arno? When the sky takes on the Pre-Raphaelite blue that so becomes it, we are reminded of the Virgin's cloak, as depicted in many a picture in the Uffizi. Old houses still stand on ramparts crumbling with age and grown over with the yellow flowers of the celandine, also called wartwort. Some of the mansions in which the great families of Languedoc were born and died are ending their lives behind the name-plates of insurance-agents and doctors; but time seems to touch the city lightly, and under the scorching heat of noon, when the streets are deserted, it looks just as in those early seventeenth century engravings that show it when the Pont Vieux was a cluster of houses, the twin of the Ponte Vecchio.

GRAPE-HARVEST AT MALROMÉ, c. 1883
Museum of Albi

In the nineteenth century Albi was still the rival of Toulouse; like Toulouse it was a sultry town, a fleshly town, and when one of its frequent thunderstorms broke, voluptuous forms decked in a froth of lingerie would come out to lean on their wrought-iron balconies. The Albigensian women were beautiful and hot-blooded, and in the summer of 1864 they offered Count Alphonse de Toulouse-Lautrec a hunting-ground that solaced him for his wife's wearisome pregnancy. The Count was a Catholic, but spent little of his time in the

Cathedral, where the Last Judgment is depicted in a series of frescoes commissioned by Louis I of Amboise from an unknown artist. He did not shudder at the vivid portrayal of the tortures suffered by lechers or see himself in the howling ranks of the 'damned'. He was a man who regretted only that the Seven Deadly Sins so magnificently illustrated here were no more than seven. He left the fear of Hell to women. His one fear was lest he might not have a son, for when thinking as a Lautrec he was interested only in males. During the night of 24th November his wish was fulfilled: while a winter storm was rattling Albi's roof-tiles, flooding its gutters and giving the whole scene an apocalyptic appearance, Countess Adèle gave birth to a fine, physically normal son. He was given the family names, Marie Raymond, like his ancestors the Counts of Toulouse, and Henri was added

GIN COCKTAIL, 1886
Museum of Albi

to these because his father was a Legitimist and that was the name of the Pretender to the throne of France. Henri Marie Raymond de Toulouse-Lautrec Monfa: a whole line in the register of births, an entire destiny as full of jolts as the progress of the carriage in which, after a week of ceremonies and celebrations, mother and baby travelled from the mansion at Albi to the Château du Bosc, the cradle and lair of a family so peculair that at the local bourgeois gatherings it was referred to only in whispers.

The château looks down across the valley of the river Viaur; the setting is admirable and the architecture pleasing, for all its rugged strength. By this time it had grown away from the fortress style of its contemporaries and become a country seat where life passed pleasantly. No-one takes the Countess de Ségur very seriously, but she did as much as Balzac and more, perhaps, than anyone else to record the family life of the French nobility in the days of *Les petites filles modèles*. For all her mincing airs, she gives a detailed description of the kitchens, the servants, the exchange of visits, the relations between masters and domestics, the whole daily round of a county family. This was the atmosphere in which Henri de Toulouse-Lautrec spent his childhood—perhaps a little less artificial, but one cannot be sure.

At the Château du Bosc lived the 'Black Prince', his sons Alphonse, Charles and Oden, with their wives and children, and a host of servants—cooks, kitchen-maids, housemaids, coachmen, and grooms and kennelmen, for there was a pack of hounds too, with stag-hunting and fox-hunting in the English manner. England set the tone in everything to do with horses and carriages—tilburys, phaetons and buggys. The neighbouring farmers supplied food for this closed-circle organization which had come down from the days when Languedoc was a Roman colony. They still belonged body and soul to the house of Lautrec, but this survival of feudalism was more in the nature of an enlightened paternalism than of a serf-and-master relationship. Be that as it may, it was in these surroundings that young Henri learnt the pride in his name which he shared with his father and carried through even the most degrading circumstances, together with the conviction of belonging to a caste set apart, not subject to the same laws or moral code as the common people. His childhood at Le Bosc left its mark on him, and it was there that he first discovered art to be his vocation.

So the 'Little Jewel'—as his grandmother used to call him because of his pretty face and slender body—was a happy child. During the summer, friends would come to visit the Lautrecs; there were games of croquet or badminton on the lawns, followed by tea out of doors, with pitchers of cream and cakes; or the company would set out in several carriages, to picnic in the nearby woods. On Sundays the chaplain came to celebrate mass and stayed to luncheon. The men would discuss hunting, for the 'Black Prince' and his three sons all shared that passion. Pierre Grèzes, the groom, also took part in the discussions, and it was he who taught Henri to ride as soon as he could walk. The little boy was fond of animals. He bred birds, and was always about the kennels or hiding in the stables. He also made toy carriages for himself: at one time he developed a collector's mania for these, besieging his cousins and friends with requests to send him miniature models from England. The evenings were spent quietly in the big drawing-room, the ladies with their embroidery and the men drawing or modelling in clay—for all three brothers had artistic talents, particularly Charles, whose sketches could well have illustrated a treatise on venery.

On 28th August 1867 Countess Adèle gave birth to Richard, Henri's brother (so named in remembrance of Richard Cœur-de-Lion, whose sister married a Lautrec), and the household gathered round the cradle with prophecies of good fortune and happiness—though by this time the Countess had few illusions about her husband's behaviour. It was in 1868 that Henri first became really aware of one kind of happy home life. His mother returned to Le Bosc after the melancholy events at Loury and was joined there by Armandine d'Alichoux de Sénégra, a delightful old maid and a distant relation, who used to supervise Henri's homework—he was having lessons with Abbé Peyre, the chaplain. Henri did just as he liked with his elderly cousin, teasing her and sometimes playing horrible practical jokes. In fact he could twist the entire household round his little finger, such was his mother's belief in his intelligence and talents.

WOMAN STANDING IN SEMI-PROFILE, 1883
Museum of Albi

SEATED NUDE, 1882
Museum of Albi

She was anxious, however, about his bone-structure, for it seemed rather fragile. Despite a huge appetite the child was not growing. His independent character asserted itself more and more, but he still had difficulty in pronouncing his words, and was hesitant of speech. He was set to study English, which he learnt with ease, and then Latin, followed by Greek. It was thought that in the comparatively rustic life at Le Bosc his chest might expand and his limbs grow sturdier.

The 1870 war broke out, and Count Alphonse hoped that the Count de Chambord would come to the throne as the result of France's defeat. When the the choice fell on a Republican system he made the best of a bad job and, once the Commune had been finally suppressed, decided to settle in Paris. Racing had been resumed, and Paris was not so far from Sologne, which offered the finest hunting in the world. Countess Adèle went too, for though all sentimental ties were severed, a man of the Count's rank and views could not adopt the new-fangled custom of divorce. As for Henri, on 1st October 1872 he became a pupil at the Lycée Fontanes in the rue du Havre (now the Lycée Condorcet). He was eight years old and eager to savour this new life, notwithstanding his delicate health and the nickname of 'P'tit bonhomme' bestowed by his classmates.

THE DECREE OF FATE

In 1872 Paris was still a town where life followed its own peaceful way. Haussmann-the-Ripper had disembowelled the area bounded by the Opera, Saint-Philippe-du-Roule, the Place de la Concorde and the Seine; but a few quiet corners had survived, and the Cité du Retiro was one of them. The carriages drove along the Faubourg Saint-Honoré, but no-one remembered the Hôtel Pérey, set back from the street at No. 30, or its stables, transformed into little houses in the romantic style. In that mansion Count Alphonse installed his family, which was quite content with this kind of retirement. The round cobblestones of the courtyard were like those of the Hôtel du Bosc at Albi, a little market was held there every morning, the house was conveniently close to Henri's school and to the rue Royale, where the dressmakers, milliners, linen-drapers and jewellers of the approaching *Belle Époque* were already setting up shop.

The Second Empire was dead, smothered in the mud of Sedan and trampled under foot in the desperate cavalry charge at Reichshoffen; but the atmosphere remained unchanged. Edmond de Goncourt notes in his diary for 11th January of this year: 'The other day, finding

SELF-PORTRAIT, 1880
Museum of Albi

MONTMARTRE: A GENTLEMAN AND TWO LADIES WITH POINTED HATS, 1886
Museum of Albi

the rue de la Paix as packed with gentlemen's carriages as if for a first night at the Théâtre Français, I was just wondering what great person's door was being thus besieged by the fashionable world, when I looked up and saw the name "Worth" inscribed above it.' Paris is still the Paris of the Empire. The names de Goncourt mentions as those of people he was in the habit of meeting include those of Ziem, the Venetian painter, Flaubert, Hugo, Théophile Gautier—who died at the end of this year—Arsène Houssaye, Zola, Courbet, the painter Regnault, Alexandre Dumas, Burty, Carpeaux the sculptor, Fantin-Latour—who had just finished his *Apotheosis of Baudelaire*—Turgeniev, and many more who have come down in history. This did not prevent him from lamenting, in his entry for 25th May, that 'Every form of aristocracy is doomed to disappear. The aristocracy of talent is now being killed by the cheap newspapers which control the fount of glory and only let it flow for those they favour. They are organizing a kind of democracy in the Republic of Letters, where the leading roles will all go to reporters or those who cook up newspapers—the only writers France will possess in fifty years' time.' This, of course, was the pronouncement of an embittered man, still grieving for the death of his brother; but it was also that of a man who felt lost in the new kind of life that was taking shape, bound up with industrial progress—one in which Thiers's conservative policy had relieved the ruling classes of all financial anxiety.

Count Alphonse de Toulouse-Lautrec, for his part, was living haughtily through this period without particularly observing its features. He belonged to the last group of great aristocrats of the Jockey Club. He rode in the Bois and distributed smiles in the Allée des Acacias, where the *demi-mondaines* by whom his son was to be so much obsessed competed in elegance with the great ladies. He was to be seen at the races—Chantilly, Longchamp, the *Prix des Drags*—in his London clothes or in some eccentric get-up. In his own circle he was renowned as a sportsman, and he revelled in his son's admiration. One day the boy must follow in his footsteps! And as he led the child to school, in his Norwegian trap with its shaggy pony, he believed that day would soon come.

At the lycée, Henri made friends with two boys who were to share in his later life. They were Louis Pascal, son of a *Préfet*, and Maurice Joyant, whose parents were rich bourgeoisie. The three engaged in friendly rivalry for school prizes, and they carried off enough of these to win them the reputation of brilliant pupils. But this period of conventional schooling was brief; it ended once and for all on 9th January 1874. Henri de Toulouse-Lautrec, too delicate for Paris, went back to Le Bosc and embarked on a round of spas, starting with Amélie-les-Bains wich was recommended for decalcification and rickets.

His return to Le Bosc brought him a sudden access of joy. He had already begun to reveal his need for constant companionship, the need to feel that he was the centre of a group that protected him and over which he could exert his influence, giving free expression to his whims. There were a great many of his cousins at Le Bosc, now that Alphonse de Toulouse-Lautrec's sister had married his wife's brother. The complete freedom of behaviour he enjoyed led the boy towards his later desire for a life lived in brothels—which was an attempt to regain this warm atmosphere, this shelter from the outside world. His amusements at Le Bosc were outdoor games, riding, hunting and cooking, together with the translation of an English book on hawking—*Falconry, its Claims, History and Practice*, by Freeman and Slavin. Jean-Jacques Rousseau would have rejoiced had he known of the wonderful success of his liberal precepts of education in the case of Henri de Toulouse-Lautrec. By the time he was fourteen the boy had a keen, penetrating intelligence, excellent taste, and a strong personality. He was a vigorous draughtsman, as can be seen from his sketches of horses, partridges and monkeys (his grandmother liked to go about with a little female monkey sitting on her shoulder), and he had written a short story entitled 'The Tale of the Pelican and the Eel' for the *Echo Français*, a short-lived paper started by Louis Pascal at the lycée.

But as though fate regretted having bestowed so many gifts on one boy—sickly as he was, and still afflicted with a terrible stammer—it struck him a warning blow on 30th May 1878, when he was thirteen-

PORTRAIT OF VINCENT VAN GOGH, 1887
Collection V. W. van Gogh, Laren

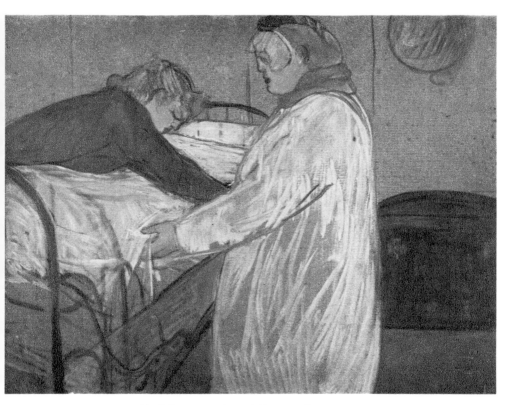

TWO WOMEN MAKING THEIR BED, 1889
Private Collection, Paris

and-a-half years old. Trying to rise to his feet from a low chair in the drawing-room of the old mansion at Albi, he fractured his left thigh-bone. This type of accident is common among old people, and its after-effects on the boy were similar: the bone was slow to mend, though it had been put into plaster at once; there was general weakness, constant fever, wasting. From that day, Countess Adèle realized that her son would never be like other boys. It was almost reassuring for her to know that what she had feared had come to pass, and at last she had a purpose in life—to nurse Henri back to health and lavish such affection on him that he would never give her the slip and return to his father. The boy was taken to Barèges, then to Nice to winter in the sun, and it was at Nice that his gift for drawing really declared itself. He used to be taken out in a little carriage, along the sea-front, and there he made quick lively sketches of the boats riding at anchor and the sailors strolling on the Promenade des Anglais.

It would of course be an exaggeration to suggest that Lautrec became a painter because he was condemned to semi-immobility. Painting had already attracted him for a long time: he had wanted to draw a bullock by way of signature on his brother's certificate of baptism; at school he had filled the margins of his exercise-books with drawings; he had gone with his father to Princeteau's studio in the Faubourg Saint-Honoré, and while at Nice he painted a *Souvenir de Chantilly* depicting himself, Princeteau and Louis Pascal galloping home from the races in a victoria. Illness was not the deciding factor in his career, it only confirmed and hastened it. When taken back to Le Bosc, the boy had begun to recover; he could walk again and was following from a distance the army manœuvres taking place near the Château, which provided him with material for countless sketches. Then fate struck a fresh blow. Out for a walk one day, Henri fell into a gulley and broke his right thighbone. That settled the matter. Lautrec never grew any taller, he developed the torso of a grown man on the legs of a small boy; and his handsome face changed gradually into a thick-lipped, monstrously masculine and sensual mask covered with black stubble.

LEARNING TO BEAR WITH ONESELF

'Happiness is never intelligent'
JEAN ROSTAND

Not one of Lautrec's letters makes the slightest allusion to the species of transformation he suffered in his fifteenth year, nor did he ever complain, or even confide in his much-loved mother or in the father he admired so greatly. Yet he was a pitiless observer and could watch in his mirror as his nose thickened, his lips began to swell, and hair sprouted on his cheeks and eventually concealed his receding chin. His chest development was comparatively enormous, so were his hands, which did not seem to belong to the arms from which they dangled. His sexual development was even more alarming, and his desires kept pace with it. He had short, bandy legs and his feet curled up like stumps. But his eyes were strangely fascinating, black and lively, though he soon became shortsighted and took to wearing pince-nez. By 1880 the transformation was complete, and Lautrec had the appearance Jules Renard described later: 'Lautrec: a tiny blacksmith with eyeglasses. A little bag with two compartments where he puts his poor legs. Thick lips, and hands like those he draws, with splayed-out, bony fingers and crescent-shaped thumbs. He often speaks of little men, with the air of saying: "I'm not so little as all that,

FIRST COMMUNION DAY, 1888
Musée des Augustins, Toulouse

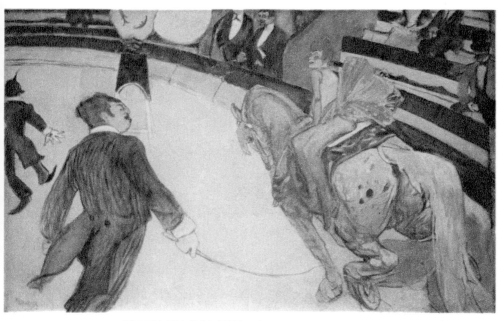

BARE-BACK RIDER AT THE CIRCUS FERNANDO, 1888
Art Institute of Chicago

myself!" At first his smallness upsets one, but then he is very lively,
very friendly; he divides his sentences by a grunt that puffs out his
lips, the way the wind blows the padding round the edge of a door,
and bubbles of saliva fly out on to his moustache . . .'

At Nice, where he went to rest after his second fracture, Lautrec
drank in the pageant of fashionable society without the slightest
resentment, and made lightning sketches of the beauties who flitted
by. Determined to overcome his handicap as far as possible, he learnt
to swim and dive, reviewed his progress day by day, and decided that
he could lead an active life, like everyone else. In 1881 he sat for the
first part of the *baccalauréat*, in Paris, failed, but passed in November at
Toulouse, though he had no intention of going to the university. In
December, he returned to Paris—and never left it again for long.

He summed himself up with perfect lucidity, and it is advisable to
do so with him, sweeping away the tinsel and false romance with

which his life has been bedizened until now. Francis Jourdain was one of his closest friends—he and Joyant, who saw Lautrec nearly every day, are the most reliable sources for any portrait. Writing fifty years after the events, Jourdain declared: 'Toulouse-Lautrec was neither a frivolous aristocrat nor an embittered buffoon, condemned to perpetual laughter. He never preached to anyone, and the thorns he was fond of displaying concealed more roses than people admitted. Bitter he was not—nor at all gloomy, nor cantankerous. Rather jovial. Those who called him bitter made the mistake of regarding his acute, uncompromising, one might even say stern realism as a lurking desire for revenge, as it were the vengeance of a cripple. Lautrec was playful, never bored and therefore never boring; he was simple, natural, and since naturalness is very rare, one might even say extraordinarily natural. He never played a part—neither that of the pathetic cripple nor that of the shrewd psychologist, caustic and disillusioned . . . Being so short of stature, he was compelled to carry his head high, and people who did not know him were inclined to attribute this to hauteur. But his entire lack of arrogance soon became evident. Lautrec was at ease in life, at ease in the relations which—from whim or accident—he maintained with men of every condition.'

Lautrec's self-scrutiny, made before he adopted Paris as his fief, was summed up in a few words to Maurice Joyant, his friend and one-time schoolfellow at Fontanes: '*One must learn to bear with oneself.*' The obvious corollary to this is that one must bear with other people, with their failings, even their mockery, and find a corner where one will not be an object of horror to anybody. And an acute psychological understanding of his fellow men seems to have been one of Lautrec's most remarkable qualities; in any gathering he infallibly singled out the person with whom he could have an enjoyable conversation. He had won the firm friendship of Louis Pascal and Maurice Joyant at school and of Devismes at Barèges; and now he quickly made friends with a man of exceptional quality, a friend of his father, who had introduced them when Henri first lived in Paris. This was Princeteau, who became his master and taught him the better part of his craft.

René Princeteau came from Libourne in the Gironde; his father is said to have been a wine-merchant. He was born deaf but had lessons from the best teachers at Bordeaux and was thoroughly versed in the etiquette of a society that made a fetish of good breeding; he was also an accomplished horseman and an outstanding gymnast. Princeteau had wished to be a sculptor and first entered the academy of his own town. But since he could well afford to live where he chose, he soon came to Paris where he was admitted to the École Impériale des Beaux-Arts, and showed himself to be gifted as a painter. He had a studio at 233 rue du Faubourg Saint-Honoré, near the Place and Avenue des Ternes, which were still almost countrified, filled with trees and gardens. He had a group of faithful collectors of his work, and many friends in sporting circles and among the beauties of the *demi-monde*. His infirmity was not an insurmountable barrier; he even went to concerts, and his speech was intelligible, though guttural. Nowadays Princeteau would be ranked with the artistic 'Establishment'; he used to show at the artists' club in the rue Volney and at the Salon, his pictures were bought by the State, and he had nothing in common with the bohemians of the Butte Montmartre. He was even snobbish enough to paint only thoroughbreds in his pictures of horses; but he had a feeling for animals, as his neighbours were the first to recognize. The cluster of houses which bore the number 233 in the Faubourg Saint-Honoré included among its residents John Lewis Brown, an Irishman from Bordeaux from whom Napoleon III used to buy equestrian pictures, and Jean-Louis Forain, then still an Impressionist but already a friend of Degas.

Princeteau welcomed Henri de Toulouse-Lautrec in the friendliest possible manner, and the 'tandem' formed by the deaf painter and the dwarf caused no mockery or studio jokes. It was based on the love of art, and Lautrec, now aged eighteen, modelled his work entirely on that of his forty-year-old friend — with so much success that in a batch of their drawings few people could say which came from which hand. Did Lautrec work on the huge heroic-sentimental depiction of the cavalry charge at Reichshoffen which was commissioned jointly from Princeteau and Poilpot? Nobody knows; but

HÉLÈNE V, MODEL IN THE STUDIO, 1888
Kunsthalle, Bremen

THE LAUNDRESS, 1888
Museum of Albi

Lautrec was becoming more and more interested in people, real people such as Forain used to sketch for the illustrated papers, to scrape a living. Lautrec did not have to worry about supporting himself; he had an allowance from his family. It was provided a little grudgingly, for the family wished he would choose a profession; but it was paid all the same, and enabled him to keep up with his friends, visiting the Circus Fernando (63 Boulevard de Rochechouart), going to the more important race meetings, and frequenting the fashionable cafés. The young man was entering the circle in which he spent the rest of his life; and a few months later, after a quite useless visit to Lamalou-les-Bains for the 'cure', he obtained the longed-for permission to study painting. His family considered that he must have a master, and through the good offices of Henri Rachou, the brother of an Albi banker, he was admitted to Bonnat's studio. This settled all Lautrec's problems. He forgot his physical condition, he could put up with himself and felt he could put up with other people; all he had to do now was to work and improve. But already, in 1879, he had painted three pictures which became famous — the *Rider trotting*, *Artilleryman saddling his Horse*, and *Chantilly Races* were all eventually bought by art galleries. His promise was being fulfilled.

BONNAT, CORMAN AND COMPANY

Bonnat
Tu peints très bien la redingote
chacun sait ça.
Tu la détaches couleur de botte
sur fond caca.

STUDIO SONG

An article in the *Courrier Français* of 2nd June 1883 might perhaps be regarded as impertinent in its attitude towards Léon Bonnat, most official of official painters, who was already a member of the Académie Française and was shortly to be awarded the Grand Cross of the Légion d'Honneur. The article in question set out to give advice to ladies on how to get their portrait painted by Bonnat. 'To be painted by Bonnat requires a preparation of prayer, fasting and every kind of austerity, for a portrait by Bonnat is a serious matter. Once you are fully imbued with a sense of the importance of the act you are contemplating, order yourself a "portrait by Bonnat" gown; there are special models. Secure a recommendation from a General, a Minister or an Ambassador; then, and only then, Monsieur Bonnat will deign to paint you, standing up, stiff as a post, sparkling like crystal, and lit from above.' Léon Bonnat, a great man of the Third Republic, was a favourite butt for journalistic humour. Some accused him of painting in mud-colours, others of putting no life into his models,

55

MAN IN A SHIRT, FROM BEHIND, 1888
Museum of Albi

JUSTINE DIEUHL, 1889-1890
Louvre, Paris

and yet others of charging too much—about one hundred thousand gold francs. But Bonnat went placidly on his way, teaching at the École des Beaux-Arts, then becoming its director, and ending his career as Chairman of the Council of Museums. At Bayonne, his birthplace, he formed a most delightful museum from his own collection, which remains to convince us, in the twentieth century, that though a bad painter he was a man of considerable taste.

In 1882 Bonnat had a kind of studio-school in the Impasse Hélène, where his pupils prepared to take the competitive entrance examination to the École des Beaux-Arts. Thither Countess Adèle sent her son every morning—or at least had him driven three days out of five—from the Hôtel Pérey where they were still living. And there Lautrec would find Rachou, of Albi, to whom he owed his introduction, Adolphe Albert, with whom he soon formed a friendship, and his stern professor, stiff in his black frock-coat and wearing high heels to increase his stature. In Bonnat's opinion Lautrec had a feeling for colour but no sense of drawing. His new pupil conscientiously washed out, rubbed out and began again, but learnt little apart from the traditional laws of composition. There is nothing surprising about Lautrec's docility; he came from an environment where confidence was inspired by anyone who was generally declared to be great and had received official honours. Lautrec genuinely admired the Salon, where Bonnat, Roll and J. P. Laurens were the leading lights. And above all, he realized that there could be no success without hard work. What did he think of Impressionism, which was flourishing by this time—for in that year, 1882, and in the Faubourg Saint-Honoré, his own district, Monet, Renoir, Pissarro, Sisley and Berthe Morisot held their seventh exhibition.

No comments on this subject have come down to us, it did not give rise to any family arguments; yet no sooner did the summer holidays arrive to release him for a few months from Bonnat's tuition, than Lautrec resumed his brighter palette in his picture *The Drinker*, the portrait of old Mathias, who sat for him at Le Bosc. Lautrec never asked questions and never confided in people. He was the perfect man of the world, living in a circle where personal problems were never mentioned — a matter of elementary good form which has reduced his many biographers to literary acrobatics and vain speculation. 'Bonnat's lash was good for me'—such was Lautrec's one admission, made many years later. It cannot be considered ridiculous, for Matisse said the same of his master at the École des Beaux-Arts and so did Rouault; and the man to whom they declared their indebtedness was Gustave Moreau, a far mòre conventional figure than Bonnat and much more tainted with cheap literature, the worst possible influence on a painter.

The year 1882 was a formative one, and so was 1883, when Lautrec studied under Cormon—Bonnat having closed his studio in order to give himself entirely to his own work and to his portrait commissions. Lautrec was glad of the change; and indeed Cormon was a man of much stronger personality. The son of a fashionable vaudeville-writer, he had studied with Cabanel and developed a passionate admiration for Gustave Doré and his fiery romanticism. After winning every possible prize at the Salon, he had now taken up prehistoric themes. His studio, in the rue Constance in Montmartre, had an atmosphere of uninhibited bohemianism which yet never clashed with the master's official side—he was world-famous, and his pupils came from as far afield as Australia and the United States. Lautrec relished the particulars of Cormon's 'legend'. In 1872, for instance, he had donned an 1830 tail-coat and celebrated his morganatic 'marriage' at the Café La Rochefoucault. Awarded the Légion d'Honneur in 1875, he had organized a procession, marching at its head with his sword, over which a joyful pupil held a protective umbrella. He professed tremendous admiration for Fromentin, and made his own excursion into orientalism with the *Death of Mahomet*. After going on to Hindu mythology, he returned to Teutonic legend with the Niebelungen. In the year when Lautrec became his pupil he was savouring the success of his *Cain*, inspired by a passage in Victor Hugo's *Légende des Siècles:* 'When with his children clad in the skins of beasts, Cain had taken flight from the eye of Jehovah . . .'

Cormon was known by the unceremonious nickname of Père La Rotule ('Swivel-joint'), because he was all skin and bone, with a flow-

AT THE NEW CIRCUS: FIVE STUFFED SHIRTS, 1891
Philadelphia Museum of Art

ing beard and bulging eyes. He corrected his pupils' work only twice a week, at top speed, and was prudent enough to refer them to Veronese and other old masters for the elucidation of problems of composition or drapery. Yet his studio was crowded. Other pupils of Bonnat, including Rachou, had gone on there; but the leader of the students was Anquetin, a giant from Normandy, three years older and sixteen inches taller than Lautrec, with rough-cast Nordic features, an iron constitution, muscles like whipcord, and an extraordinary gift for drawing and for horsemanship. Anquetin appointed himself Lautrec's protector, sheltering him from horseplay and practical jokes and, most important of all, giving him confidence in his talent. Anquetin had no doubts as to his own abilities; he was convinced that he would become one of the world's great painters. The other friends Lautrec made in Cormon's studio included Charles Edouard Lucas, Lampier, and René Grenier, a jovial man from Toulouse who was to play an important part in Lautrec's life when, before long, he grew weary of the family atmosphere in the Cité du Retiro.

Apart from his apprenticeship to painting, studio attendance had various drawbacks for Lautrec, including that of lowering the barriers of his private life. Everybody at Cormon's, apart from Lautrec, had at least one mistress, but when Charles Edouard Lucas thrust Marie Charlet into his arms the cure was perhaps more terrible than the complaint. Marie Charlet was a 'flower of the streets'—to use the phraseology current on the Butte Montmartre, which was then a kind of moral no-man's-land. She was sixteen years old, flat-chested, with full lips and big coal-black eyes, a nymphomaniac, and since being introduced to love-making by her father, a drunkard who lived in the rue Mouffetard, she had roamed Paris in a permanent state of hysteria. She called Lautrec her 'darling coat-hanger', regaled the whole district with descriptions of the nights they spent together despite his diminutive height, and brought to him, with no sign of jealousy, such of her girl-friends as were in need of affection. She made no attempt to obtain money from Lautrec or to gain a hold over him, though she must have suspected he was richer than his friends. She tired of him as abruptly as she had taken him up.

RED-HAIRED WOMAN, 1891
Museum of Albi

Lautrec's association with Marie Charlet convinced him that while he was a man like any other, he could hope for nothing more from love than a parody, the satisfaction of his physical needs, and that for affection he must look solely to his mother, Countess Adèle, who watched over him day after day, trying to spare him fatigue and nervous tension, to soothe his feverish zest for life and wean him away from the nightly round of questionable pleasures. Why should love be bound up with physical appearance? Lautrec constantly asked

RED HAIRED WOMAN SEEN FROM BEHIND, 1891
Museum of Albi

himself this, for at eighteen years old he had an extraordinary longing to open his heart, and his mind was full of Jeanne d'Armagnac, a pretty cousin who had kept him company when he was at Barèges.

During this period his work was developing by leaps and bounds. At the studio he followed Cormon's advice conscientiously, but did not give his whole attention to it. He took up the conventional subjects that were suggested: *Icarus*, *Scenes from Merovingian Life*, *The Sacred Grove*—this last a species of allegory in the style of Puvis de Chavannes's *Sacred Grove*. But he felt more at ease with the nude in *Fat Maria* or with *Cart in the Mud*.

It was in the summer holidays of 1884, at Malromé, a few miles from Langon, where the Countess had bought a property of some hundred and twenty-five acres to be nearer to her cousins the Pascals, that Lautrec sifted out what he had learnt from what he himself felt. He had made one last attempt at a landscape and then reverted to portrait-painting, convinced that in the final resort he was only interested in people, with their burden of spirit and flesh and the stories of their minds. Life went on quietly in the turretted château behind its screen of trees. Affectionately but clear-sightedly, noting the traces time had left on her face, he painted his mother at breakfast, sitting deep in thought at the table on which the only glint of white light comes from a china cup. This picture is like a last caress from his childhood. For his mind was now made up. On returning to Paris he would spread his wings, even if he burnt them!

MONTMARTRE

'Toulouse-Lautrec is a Baron who has taken root in a brothel
ANDRÉ SUARÈS

Montmartre as it was around 1885 can still be seen in the pictures
painted by Michel, for change was slow in coming to the hill—which
was to become a place of pilgrimage, thanks to a great exercise of
imagination in the interests of the tourist industry. The Butte was
originally a village among market-gardens and flour-mills, a favourite
goal of lovers on their Sunday outing, a hiding-place for unmarried
mothers and wide boys, a lucky dip for professional foster-mothers
and the Waifs and Strays Society, and a refuge for lovers of silence
and the rustic scene. It began to be 'colonized' from the base upwards,
in concentric circles, the peak being reserved for the Sacré-Cœur, that
monstrosity, beloved only of Utrillo, which commemorates the defeat
of 1870. Though it had become part of Paris shortly before that war,
Montmartre still asserted its independance by fostering a slightly
individual atmosphere, a psychology tinged with anarchy, alien both
to the bourgeois artists of the neighbouring Batignolles on one side,
and to the unleavened proletariat of Ménilmontant and Belleville on
the other. Two wide streets, the rue Lepic and the rue des Martyrs,
drew off the future population of Montmartre towards the slopes

THE MORNING AFTER, 1889
Museum of Albi

where the line of the funicular had already been marked out, and for
a long time the tide rose no higher than what were then the 'outer'
boulevards, where it swirled round certain bastions such as the
'Grande Pinte', the 'Plus grand Bock', the 'Auberge du Clou', the
'Chat Noir' and the 'Elysée Montmartre'.

Lautrec's acquaintance with Montmartre had so far been restricted
to Cormon's studio in the rue Constance, a turning off the rue Lepic,
the rue Ganneron, where Rachou lived, and the avenue de Clichy
where Anquetin lived. But when he went to share a flat with his
friend Grenier, at 19b rue Fontaine, he at last had time to explore
what was henceforth to be his 'hunting-ground'.

ARISTIDE BRUANT ON HIS BICYCLE, 1892
Museum of Albi

Grenier was fond of Lautrec, though he had a poor opinion of his painting, which baffled him. Grenier had money, his parents owned a lot of property in the Ternes district and made him an allowance of twelve thousand francs, enough for him to enjoy life himself and still leave a well-filled purse, as well as complete freedom of conduct, to his wife Lily—an ex-model of Degas, a buxom, freckled redhead. Grenier was not jealous, either of his wife or of other artists' talents, being confident that his work was as good as theirs. He was a jovial night-bird, always ready to arrange a fancy-dress ball, a dinner-party or a nocturnal tour of Paris; and though Toulouse-Lautrec was not insensitive to Lily's charms he took care to keep the fact to himself to avoid upsetting the family atmosphere that suited him. He was still going to Cormon's studio, painting as much as he could and drawing even more; his hand had grown surer, and the bold lines of his work wrung a half-compliment from the exacting Degas.

What charmed Lautrec about Montmartre was not so much the setting as the inhabitants. MacOrlan, the only born story-teller to have attempted a life of him, gives a picture of Montmartre: 'In front of Lautrec's studio,' he writes, 'lay the celebrated *maquis* which took up all one side of the rue Caulaincourt, from the rue Tourlaque to the rue Girardon, behind the Moulin de la Galette. It was an expanse of little houses and wooden huts, lying among lilacs, seringa-bushes, hen-coops rabbit-hutches, fences and patches of hay. Good and bad were mingled in this *maquis*. Art students lodged side by side with libertarian rag-pickers, and harlots came there in quiet moments to pick up the occupations of their long-lost country child hood. Few Parisians went to the Butte Montmartre in those days. At night it might seem dangerous, and often was so indeed, for the riff-raff occupied a few strategic points where "affairs of honour" were settled with every prospect of a successful flight when a policeman's whistle brought up reinforcements. A perverse, entirely literary and picturesque love of danger developed in this little known Montmartre which lay off the beaten track of song and humour. Bruant cast it into a literary mould that was profound in its simplicity. And the artist's infatuation with the nocturnal figures of the Montmartre—

ARISTIDE BRUANT AT LES AMBASSADEURS, 1892
Museum of Albi

and, more generally, Parisian—underworld now appeared for the first time, perhaps, in the history of art.'

A leading member of Montmartre society was Rodolphe Salis, the 'gentleman taverner'. For years, Salis had been the embodiment of failure, a cartoonist with no talent, an engraver with no medals, an archaeologist with no excavations; until the day when it occurred to him to imitate the proprietor of La Grande Pinte by opening a *cabaret-chantant*. This he did in a former post office in the Boulevard Rochechouart, naming it 'Le Chat Noir'. His second good idea was to persuade the Club des Hydropathes, the members of which were Alphonse Allais, Émile Goudeau, Jules Jouy, Jean Moréas, MacNab, Maurice Donnay, Richepin, Charles Cros, Rollinat and (transiently) Verlaine, to desert the Left Bank, settle down in his tavern with its sham Louis XIII decoration, and provide the entertainment. The business soon began to make a profit; the cream of Paris society crowded into these cramped quarters to drink bad beer and enjoy rubbing shoulders with the rabble and watching the women of easy virtue pick up customers, while MacNab reeled off his songs amid the smoke of half-Havanas. Lautrec went to the Chat Noir to enjoy the noise and the contrasting lights, but found it altogether too 'phoney'. However, when Salis sold his goodwill to Aristide Bruant and the little place was renamed 'Le Mirliton', things were different. Aristide Bruant was genuine, another type of man altogether. Physically he was tall and powerfully-built, clean-shaven (unusual in those days), with a Roman profile and a voice described by Jules Lemaitre as one 'for riots and barricades'. At the time of opening the Mirliton he was thirty-five. He came of Gâtinais peasant stock, had affinities with Sologne and thus with Beauce, but as a boy he had been brought to Paris by his drunken father and a neurasthenic mother—and left to fend for himself. Loving the country as he did, he had to find work as a lawyer's office-boy and later as a railway clerk. This atmosphere grew too stifling, and he decided to try his luck in the *cabarets*, going from one to another to recite other people's verses. In the endless tramping about that his poverty made inevitable, his wanderings from one lodging to the next, he discovered the human sewer-rats who lived in the outskirts of Paris, lurking in the waste land where the fortifications had been dismantled, in the slums that were beginning to rise in the far side of Clichy and towards the Porte d'Italie. MacNab, Alphonse Allais, Jules Jouy and the rest were bourgeois; Bruant was proletarian, conscious of his condition and of the reason for it. His outlook was not the same as theirs, he lived on the edge of society and he was bent on vengeance. He saw clearly, and Lautrec saw eye to eye with him: the prostitute, the gangster, the judge, the executioner, the livid dawn, the wet street, the hollow chest, the rings under the eyes, the feverish hand clutching the edges of the cape... Bruant could express all this with poignant accuracy, because he spoke the language of that world. Lautrec had no wish to reform society. He was not one of the aristocrats who posed as revolutionaries. But if society was rotting, if the mildewspots of evil were to be seen everywhere, acceptance was as good a rule as any, and then one's own circumstances became much less important and one's sufferings diminished. Since others are unhappy, the victims of injustice, one's own wretchedness is relieved, the injustice one suffers seems easier to bear. Invective becomes a powerful antidote, and Bruant taught Lautrec that invective was an art.

The Mirliton was always packed. New arrivals were greeted with stinging comment, women being hailed as *linges* (dressed-up tarts) and men as 'pimps' or 'bums'; everyone leaving was sped with a couplet including the word 'cochon'. But when Bruant climbed on a table to sing *Nini Peau de chien* or *A Saint-Lazare* it seemed as though this lament from the depths of human misery must surely move the most indifferent, and perhaps change their behaviour.

> *Tas d'inachevés tas d'avortons*
> *Fabriqués avec des viandes veules,*
> *Vos mèr's avaient donc pas d'tétons,*
> *Qu'a's ont pas pu vous fair' des gueules?*

Bruant had long admired Steinlen, who had been the first to do his portrait—about the same time as Desboutins, an engraver who is

PORTRAIT OF ÉMILE BERNARD, 1885
Collection Arthur Jeffress, London

now forgotten because he went away, settled in Rome, and became more interested in ancient stones than in people. Bruant now admired Lautrec. Maurice Donnay mentions that whereas everyone else who came in was greeted with abuse, Bruant would hail Lautrec by shouting: 'Silence, gentlemen, here comes the great painter Toulouse-Lautrec, with one of his friends and a pimp I don't know.' Was it Bruant who first introduced Lautrec to brothels? The question has often been asked and never answered, but it was undoubtedly Bruant who took the painter to the house in the rue de la Chapelle, considered in those days as a 'knocking-shop' of the lowest order, where for a few pence the women would entertain the navvies who frequented it and who were usually drunk.

Lautrec never sentimentalized the prostitute's lot. He considered that people did as they wanted, that the slippery slope could be avoided, and that vice had its own attraction for some. The writer to whom he was most akin was not Zola but Maupassant, as much the aristocrat and towards the end of his life as physically handicapped as Lautrec himself.

Apart from the Mirliton, Lautrec often went to the Clou in the Boulevard Trudaine, whose proprietor was also a friend of his, and in fact to all the cafés within a certain limited area which included the 'Général Moncey' in the Avenue de Clichy, the 'Guerbois'—a favourite with the Impressionists—the Café des Arts, the Café de l'Ermitage, the Cafés de l'Orient, de la Poste and des Entrepreneurs, the Café Fontaine which was nearest to the home of his friends the Greniers, the 'Grand Bock' and the Café des Colonnes. He would go to any of these to drink a glass of absinthe or vermouth with his fellow-students, or by himself in moments of depression, when he felt in need of the bracing of alcohol. He spent hours on café terraces, watching the endless bustle in the street, noting a gesture, a dress, a smile, the glimpse of a stocking when a skirt was held up. When he had gazed his fill he would go down to the bottom of the rue Caulaincourt, where a photographer friend of his, Forest, allowed him to use a little house in a garden. There he painted and drank, 'little but often.' He painted and made love, for he had found the ideal

ENGLISHMAN AT THE MOULIN ROUGE, 1892
Museum of Albi

model—no prude, but intelligent for once. This was Marie Clémentine Valadon, alias Suzanne, alias Maria, who worked for a washerwoman in the rue Tourlaque and was the mother of an illegitimate child now three years old. She had begun by posing for Puvis de Chavannes, in his Place Pigalle studio, when she brought him his laundry. Then, in 1883, she had sat for Renoir, and later for Zaudomeneghi, a Venetian, who introduced her to Lautrec. In his portrait of her she has a brilliant complexion, but her lips are compressed, her

PORTRAIT OF THE ACTOR HENRY SAMARY, 1889
Collection Jacques Laroche, Paris

chin juts out, and her expression is sullen and infinitely secretive. When making love she threw off all restraint; but she never confided in Lautrec, never told him that she, too, painted, or at any rate made drawings, never mentioned her little boy, Maurice Utrillo, or his father (but she may not have known who that had been); she was reserved and stubborn. True, Lautrec did not encourage confidences, since he was not eager to reciprocate them. Was he melancholy, or gay, kind or malicious? He was simply Lautrec, like a character in a play, with the liveliest pencil in Montmartre and the strongest head; the most tireless of the local nightbirds.

The plumes of train-smoke rose above the Batignolles cutting; houses were going up in all directions in Montmartre, for 1885 was a prosperous year and Paris was on the move northward and westward; the ladies of the town were accommodating, and drink flowed in torrents. At the end of that year came Lautrec's twenty-first birthday. What about love? He would reply: 'And what about the bawdy houses? You wouldn't want them to go bust?' He took Candide's view that all was for the best in the best of all possible worlds.

Seeking for Lautrec's antecedents in painting we have a wide choice. The earliest was perhaps Callot; nearer to Lautrec's own time were Gavarni, with his pictures of young wantons, and Constantin Guys, who painted bawds in brothels, sailors on the spree and light ladies driving in their carriages. As MacOrlan points out, Guys shows girls who are amiable, wily, self-possessed and roguish, whereas Lautrec's women are preyed upon by the demon of the streets, corroded by the idleness of the men who are their masters. They live like small animals stubbornly reticent in the shadow of murder. 'Death never appears in Lautrec's work,' notes MacOrlan. 'He no doubt disliked alluding to that final word. But it stands behind the women he paints or draws, from *Fat Maria* (1884) to *Red Rosa* (1888), with her white camisole and her rat-like face.'

A CHOICE OF FRIENDS

The nice thing about the Greniers was their hospitable spirit, even though red-haired Lily — Lily la Rousse — came to be nicknamed 'Lily la Rosse' by Lautrec in allusion to her tactlessness (she had a habit of criticizing everyone mercilessly in the sincere belief that her remarks were complimentary). Lily delighted in Lautrec's company; he was always ready for any expedition she might suggest. She easily persuaded him to visit her husband and herself in the country, at Villiers-sur-Morin, where they had a little house.

Lautrec was not fond of the country, except at Le Bosc and Malromé. He expresses this in the only sentence he ever composed for a book he and Cipa Godebsky were planning to write together: 'It is in the country that one becomes conscious of celibacy.' But he went to the Greniers', other members of the company being his painter friends Anquetin and Louis Legrand. The latter's talent had a certain resemblance to that of Degas, and in course of time he achieved due recognition in the history of art. In those days, getting to Villiers was quite an undertaking; by train as far as Esbly and then on by stage-coach, which took the whole morning to cover the distance. The

THE DANCE AT THE MOULIN ROUGE, 1890
Collection Henry P. McIlhenny, Philadelphia

village consisted of a few houses, the most prominent being the inn, kept by a certain Ancelin. Francis Jourdain tells us that: 'Lautrec soon began to appreciate the charm of Villiers, the Bout de Paille, Contevrault, the Bois de Misère, and the meadows carpeting the gentle hills at the top of which the villages of Dainville and Mont-barbin formed clusters of pretty houses. He waxed bucolic, writing that he wished he were a faun and could walk naked in the woods.' But this neophyte in the woodland world was a townsman and bore-dom soon seized him. Lautrec saw no significance in the movement of branches, and rapidly grew weary of the multicoloured fields that spread like a charming Harlequin's cloak with the clouds drifting

PREPARING FOR THE QUADRILLE, 1892
National Gallery of Art, Washington, D.C.

above them. He had no wish to imitate his friends, who scattered about the neighbourhood and stood in front of their easels, gazing at the landscape through half-closed eyes. He went back to the inn, had a barrel rolled up to the largest of the four walls of the room, and began to paint on that. But he did not paint what he had just seen ; he painted what he was sorry not to be seeing at present and would soon be seeing again—what he was momentarily deprived of, but was 'born' to paint, as the saying is. He painted a deceptively gilded setting lit by gas-lamps, where ballet dancers with made-up faces were dancing and the comically hairy hand of the conductor loomed in the foreground. On the left-hand door Lautrec painted a 'barker' —the name given to the call-boy who went round behind the scenes of a theatre before the curtain rose, clanging a bell to summon the performers to the stage. Above the door he painted a group of fire-men on duty in the theatre he had made.

The inn room was ugly and rather dark, but now Lautrec had trans-formed it. Its dusky atmosphere sparkled with the light so eagerly sought by the painter's eyes. Lautrec was himself again ; in Ancelin's country inn his memory had reconstructed one of those spectacles he would never tire of watching.

Anquetin deliberately refrained from advising Lautrec in his work, but another of Cormon's pupils took upon himself to do so. This was Émile Bernard, Lautrec's junior by four years, and filled with the sacred fire. Dissatisfied with his teacher's lessons, he was organiz-ing a rebellion against what he called 'faking' — by which he meant the tricks of scumbling, blending, and, in short, everything that the vocabulary of the Beaux-Arts included under the word 'technique' to demonstrate his point, he took Anquetin, Lampier and Lautrec to visit a seller of artists' materials known as Le Père Tanguy, who had pictures by Cézanne in his shop in the rue Clauzel. These would launch Bernard into long discourses on colour, in which he would also refer to the Impressionists who were showing at Durand-Ruel's gallery in the rue Laffitte. Theorizing always bored Lautrec, but having asked Émile Bernard to pose for him, he had ample op-portunity to listen. He listened and smiled, through the twenty sittings he needed before the portrait was finished. Bernard, the obstinate controversialist, came on foot every morning from his home at Asnières to vent his ill-humour in Cormon's studio. In the end Cormon threw him out, and he went to join Gauguin at Pont-Aven.

Lautrec had been struck by the Impressionists' use of colour, and still more by their free style of composition. At this period Pissarro was declaring in his letters that the painter must not try to discover a formula, must not let himself be influenced by clever pupils, must not set out with ready-made intensions; in short, he must learn to see things with his own eyes and work without preconceived system. He added that it was better to work in the direction of caricature than to turn out 'pretty pictures'. Lautrec was on Pissarro's side without knowing him; but this may have been due to the influence of Degas, whom he admired though he did not like him.

At the age of fifteen, Lautrec had come across *Miss Lola*, a painting in which Degas shows the girl trapezist at the Circus Fernando hanging from the roof of the circus by her teeth. What he liked about it was the style of composition, which he recognized later in *Green room at the Opera* and the *Ballet of 'Robert le Diable'*. But apart from this he had nothing in common with Degas's attitude. Degas was an embittered man, a conventional, reactionary bourgeois, malicious towards other people, and timid as well. He went in continual fear of a revolution, had no sympathy for the humbler classes, and loathed women above all things. Degas haunted a few rather snobbish drawing-rooms, a few families, preferably rich ones, and took no interest whatever in the street scene. Lautrec described him, in Bruant's slang, as a *bande à froid*, though he could not fail to respect the gift for incisive expression that Degas revealed in every line he drew.

As well as Anquetin and Émile Bernard, Lautrec now had another daily companion—Vincent Van Gogh. To the rest of the little group, Vincent seemed quite old. He was already thirty-five when he entered Cormon's studio, where he began to work with furious energy, but in his own way, which consisted of completely transforming whatever was put in front of him. He slashed bold lines across his canvas, splashed it with blue and yellow, made of it a kind of St Vitus's

LA GOULUE ENTERING THE MOULIN ROUGE, 1892
Collection Dr and Mrs David M. Levy, New York

AT THE MOULIN ROUGE, 1892
Art Institute of Chicago

dance that left Cormon flabbergasted but silenced. He was unlike
anyone else, and Lautrec sensed in him a man of his own mettle, at
odds with a world inimical to people who did not belong. What
made Vincent an outcast was his material and even more his moral
distress — rejected love, religion which had shown only its hostile,
oppressive aspect, misunderstanding in his own circle. Vincent had
a brother, Theo, who was running the Boussod & Valadon gallery
in the Boulevard Montmartre. Lautrec went there with Vincent and

looked at the stacked canvases, but he made no comment. He painted Vincent's portrait as he had done Bernard's, and brought out his friend's 'rhapsodical' side; but he shunned his theories about painting, his missionary aspect, and firmly refused to join the community of artists Van Gogh wanted to establish. In point of fact Van Gogh made him uncomfortable, and his lack of reticence jarred on him. Never were two men more unlike — the one proclaiming a fervour of love, imbued with a reformer's zeal, the other silent and withdrawn. One was a kind of apostle aspiring to martyrdom, the other a dilettante, looking on at life with amusement, condemning nothing. Lautrec gave Van Gogh the friendly advice to move south, towards the light; this counsel was not followed until later.

The fact is that none of Lautrec's companions captivated him to the point of influencing him in any way, not one of them surmounted the barrier of his reserve. Lautrec was a solitary; he enjoyed living in the middle of society on condition that society would leave him in peace. A sociable egoist who bore his sufferings in secret—utterly unlike Gauguin, who poured out his troubles.

For a time Lautrec shared the studio of his friend Rachou, at 22 rue Ganneran. Rachou lived on until 1944. After years of bohemianism he became curator of the museum at Toulouse. He was the first man in Paris to get one of Lautrec's pictures into a public collection. He was a good painter, who attracted notice at the Salon, and a writer and dramatist as well. Gémier staged a play by him at the Théâtre de la Renaissance. Next Lautrec moved to Gauzi's studio at 7 rue Tourlaque. Montmartre seemed to have more pretty women than any other district, and now he was captivated by another redhead, Carmen Gaudin, whom he persuaded to sit for him, believing her to be 'a formidable bitch'; she proved to be a sweet-natured girl, destined to an uneventful career as a good model. He did four portraits of her, the finest of which (now in the Knoedler collection) has affinities with Rembrandt. Did he make love to her? There is not the slightest trace of any love-affair during that year; it was, however, the year of Lautrec's real discovery of the music-hall as a subject for painting, and perhaps of the crystallization of his genius.

EARLY SUCCESS

A dark street. The gas-lamps cast yellowish rings of light on the wet, slippery cobbles. Cabs jolt slowly along the boulevard; shadowy figures glide past behind the trees, keeping close to the house-fronts. Prostitutes stand in corners, fidgeting from one foot to the other as the drizzling rain settles in sparkling beads on their moth-eaten feather boas. A pimp is leaning against the wall with a cigarette dangling from his lip, just as Steinlen's pencil has so often caught him. He touches his cap with a perfunctory gesture as Henri de Toulouse-Lautrec hobbles by on his short legs, with his glasses steamed over, his tiny cane grasped in his right hand and his bowler hat on the back of his head. He is on his way to the *café-concert*.

There were over twenty *'Caf' Conc'* in Paris in 1888. They bore such names as Eldorado, Alcazar, Scala, Horloge, Concert-Parisien, Eden, Ba-ta-clan, Pépinière, Cigale, Ambassadeurs, Alcazar d'Été, Européen, Divan Japonais. Their vogue might last for several months, or they might fade out for no apparent reason. It was a question of district and atmosphere. Unlike the *cabaret-chantant*, such as Salis's Chat Noir or Bruant's Mirliton, the *'Caf' Conc'* had a stage, with foot-

THE CABARET SINGER ARISTIDE BRUANT, 1892
Museum of Albi

lights and a curtain. It was almost a theatre, not quite a music-hall.
Lautrec pushes through the door of one of them. Inside, at first, one
could see nothing, a white cloud hovers halfway to the ceiling. A
smell of strong tobacco, cheap scent, dress-preservers, close-packed
humanity and sour beer fills the nostrils of the new arrival, fresh from
a street where the damp air smells of horse-dung and plane-tree
leaves—not, as yet, of petrol. A tinny piano is strumming the tune of
a romantic ballad, *Mon cœur est une fleur d'automne* . . . The red-gowned

REINE DE JOIE, 1892
Museum of Albi

singer raises a hand to her heavily-rouged cheek, bows her head and
bends forward, displaying her heavy bosom. The audience joins in
the chorus: '*Vous l'avez pris, je vous le donne, tout sim-ple-ment!*' Lautrec
wipes his pince-nez, sits down at one of the marble-topped tables,
and surveys the scene. 'One has to make it clear', writes Francis
Jourdain, 'that stage-lighting in those days had one peculiarity. The
performers were lit almost solely from the footlights. Rising from
below in this way (coming, that is, in the opposite direction from

sunshine or the glow of a chandelier), the light gave them a completely different aspect, masking their faces, as it were, with greenish dusk, entirely changing them, bringing out hitherto unsuspected features.' This was what interested Lautrec—this strange light, moulding the performers' faces, exaggerating their gestures, turning their attempts at pathos to ridicule. The words were of little importance—soldiers' songs, love-songs, patriotic songs (people were already anticipating the return of Alsace-Lorraine to France), or bawdy, it made no odds; what counted for Lautrec was the look of the place, the fantastic picture it presented. To quote his constant companion, Jourdain, again: 'Just as some people are enriched by what they hear, Lautrec was enriched by what he saw. He lived through his eyes. He believed only in what he saw. He nourished his mind on what he looked at, as no-one else was capable of looking. He put the most subtle intelligence into the act of watching, but that intelligence was heedless of everything except the creature who was being glowered at, pursued, held in sight, hunted down and trapped by his unwavering stare. The theatrical illusion an audience demands, and which the actor's art is wholly directed towards creating, was something against which Lautrec never needed to struggle; it had no hold over that dyed-in-the-wool materialist.'

Lautrec was obsessed with movement, that was why static landscape had no attraction for him; and he sought it out in another setting as well—the public dance-hall. The first of these places that he visited was naturally the Elysée-Montmartre, close to the Chat Noir; here the star turn was the so-called 'naturalistic quadrille'. Then, never satisfied with just one show, he went to the Moulin de la Galette, at the top of the rue Lepic. There he found a quite different public, paying two *sous* a head for the right to waltz in a glass-covered enclosure. Counter-jumpers, laundresses, milliners, servant-girls, women from the factories (there were factories already in the Batignolles district), prostitutes and their bullies — all the world's misery in a whirl of flounces and the smell of sweat. The women were bareheaded (the three in the foreground of the picture he painted in 1889 have splendid manes of hair piled on their heads), the men wore

THE MOULIN ROUGE. LA GOULUE, 1891
Museum of Albi

their hats, in the manner of the loafers of that day. Lautrec was not there to criticize, rules were beneath him, life was a show and nothing else.

The great discovery he was to make in this motley world, one which helped him to overcome the difficulty he still found in summing up this dance-hall and music-hall atmosphere on canvas, was a little Alsatian girl fresh from her native province, Louise Weber, nick-named 'la Goulue' ('greedy-guts'). A laundress by trade, she had been taken to the Circus Médrano by Marcel Astruc and gone from there to the Moulin de la Galette. An article published in *Gil Blas* described her as follows: 'Short, pink-cheeked, baby-faced, plump. From a low-cut, dark dress there shot forth pearly shoulders and a saucy face, crowned by thick golden hair coiled so high that it resembled the crest of a helmet. The moment she began to dance her cheeks glowed, unruly locks broke loose, her arms rose, her legs swung up, beating the air, threatening the spectators' hats, drawing their eyes to her swirling petticoats and embroidered drawers. As the figures of the quadrille succeed one another, she alternates the tantalizing arching of her belly with a lascivious wriggle of the hips slowly concluding a *bouillonnement*, she reveals a little patch of real, bare skin just above the garter. And from that scrap of rosy skin a scorching ray darts out, like incandescent steel, to strike the breath-less spectators.' The girl's nickname was given her because she emptied any glass that stood forgotten on a table, had an enormous appetite and a flow of filthy language; yet when dancing she was transfigured. It was this transfiguration that mystified Lautrec and captivated him, this process he wanted to record, together with the action of the sorcerer who had perhaps made it possible—Valentin le Désossé, La Goulue's partner and her instructor in the quadrille.

Lautrec used Valentin le Désossé as an alibi if anyone reproached him for keeping low company. 'But he's a notary,' he would protest. 'A notary isn't low company!' In fact it was Valentin's father who was a notary, at Sceaux. The son had studied law, but had then fled from his too peaceful suburban home and set up as a wine-merchant in the rue Coquillière by day and leader of the dance at the Bal Mabille by night. Being a shrewd man all the same, he bought houses near the École Militaire and let them to army officers, who would greet him with due courtesy when they met him in the Bois, wearing his perpetual top-hat, with the fag end of a *cigarillo* projecting from his gap-toothed slit of a mouth. Little by little, the denizens of the public dance-halls grew extraordinarily important to Lautrec; he became part and parcel of their world and henceforth experienced from within everything he transposed, in a style of ever-increasing freedom and mordancy, into the brilliant paintings to which he soon added—discovering them with supreme delight—the resources of lithography, and particularly poster work.

For two years (since 1886) Lautrec had been drawing for the press, particularly for the *Courrier Français*, of which Jules Roques was director. He belonged to a team that included Lunel, Legrand, Steinlen, Willette and Forain. In that same year, under the pseudonym of 'Tolau-Segroeg', he had sent a picture to the *Salon des Arts Incohérents*—No. 323 of the catalogue, described as *The Batignolles three-and-a-half years BC*, oil painting on emery paper. In 1889, under the same name (Tolau-Segroeg being described as 'A Hungarian of Montmartre, who has visited Cairo and lodges with one of his friends in the Rue Yblas, under the third gas-lamp on the left, a pupil of Pubis de Cheval, specializing in family groups with yellow or pastel backgrounds') he sent in *Portraits of an unfortunate family afflicted with 'petite grêlure'*. This fact, first pointed out by Jean Adhémar, shows that Lautrec was absolutely at one with the world of artists, although he was apt to grit his teeth spitefully and lacked Forain's instinct for the stinging caption that would go with a particular drawing. Studies of environment suited him best. He published some in Bruant's short-lived publication *Mirliton* and in *Paris Illustré*, but on a very small scale, like the black-and-white lithographs he tried to sell to certain dealers—Kleinmann, Pellet, and Segot. Always at the back of his mind was a remark made by René Martin, art critic of the *Figaro*: 'More talent goes into a poster than into many pictures that make a sensation.' Chéret, hailed by Félix Fénéon as 'the double-colombier Tiepolo', had a triumphant exhibition of his posters at the

THE POLICEMAN'S DAUGHTER, 1890
Kunsthalle, Hamburg

Potinière. Lautrec decided to do posters, but he wanted a studio of his own first of all. At last he secured his family's permission and enough money to rent a third-floor studio at 27 rue Caulaincourt, at the corner of the rue Tourlaque. He went back at night to the flat he shared with Dr Bourges, at 19 rue Fontaine, and thus remained close to the Greniers, who were still his faithful friends.

He was beginning to take firm root as a painter. He was invited by the 'Groupe des XX' to show at Brussels, and Theo Van Gogh took several of his pictures for Boussod & Valadon. Octave Mauss, the founder of the Groupe des XX, sent Van Rysselberghe to Paris to look at Lautrec's work. He was enthusiastic, and the Belgian group rubbed their hands in satisfaction at the prospect of shocking the conventional-minded yet again. But curiously enough, it was Lautrec's eleven paintings which won the most praise from the critics, who dealt severely with Signac and James Ensor.

Lautrec had never been happier in his work. *At the Moulin de la Galette* and *The Elysée-Montmartre* could stand up to comparison with Degas' best paintings. *The Quadrille of the Louis XIII Chair* struck him already as old-fashioned stuff. He was seized by a positive fury for painting. Inducing his friend Gauzi—a native of Toulouse, whom he had met at Cormon's and who now had the studio next to his— to pose for him, he produced *First Communion Day* (page 48), a sort of caricature of the typical bourgeois family. It shows Gauzi, in an opera-hat, pushing a perambulator; behind him walks a little girl dressed for her First Communion and looking 'like a cream cheese'; behind her, again, comes her mother, dragging a smaller girl by the hand. All the tedium of a bourgeois Sunday in Paris is reflected in the weary attitudes of these different characters. But the painting entitled *Masked Ball* is full of life, and *Red Rosa*, with her hair hanging over her face and her hands dangling at her sides, half slattern, half animal, in a loose-fitting blouse that makes a patch of dazzling brightness against the dark background, strikes one like a blow in the face. Lautrec had caught syphilis from Red Rosa, the carotty-haired girl from Montrouge, but he found her attractive all the same, and did several portraits of her, including *Red-haired Woman in a White Jacket*.

WOMAN CROUCHING, 1893
Museum of Albi

Valadon was still his official mistress, however, and his favourite model. In the latter capacity she sat for one of the finest pictures he painted during this period—*The Morning After* (page 66). Sitting at a table in front of a bottle of red wine and a glass, propped on her elbows, her head resting on one hand, the woman stares into space, pursuing some vague dream. In her role of mistress she led Lautrec a dance and even faked a suicide attempt. But this was her last ruse, for he had grown tired of her lies, her escapades, her spiteful remarks and perpetual bad temper—and tired of her mother, a deliberate troublemaker—and he dropped her for good. He consoled himself with drink, and with watching La Goulue dance. How was he to represent her frenzied movements, those flashes of white linen? Feverishly, he made sketch after sketch.

Sketches of another model were heaping up too. This was a young woman of a wealthy family who had fallen in love with her riding-

94

THE BALLET 'PAPA CHRYSANTHÈME', 1892
Museum of Albi

master, left home for his sake, and was now a circus rider. Lautrec had seen her at the Circus Fernando; she had consented to come to the rue Tourlaque and pose for him, and the result was a vast number of studies, in boldly cross-hatched lines, done with turpentine wash on plain cardboard. From this mass of studies Lautrec made one large canvas, *Bare-back Rider at the Circus Fernando* (page 49). In this, finally, the most prominent figure turned out to be Monsieur Loyal, the ringmaster, with his whip. He alone shows up in the ring, the equestrienne being no more than a red-haired girl sitting sideways on a sturdy horse ; the horse's back follows the curve of the ringside seats, and his plumy tail echoes her pale green tutu.

Lautrec seems to have worked without pause, for the canvases were piling up in the studio—which was in any case cluttered with a variety of ill-assorted objects, such as old helmets and lengths of material. A 'period' cabinet stood open, revealing a jumble of ballet shoes, old newspapers, Persian ceramics (a present from Count Alphonse), dumb-bells, soda-water siphons, the kakomonos that had been Lautrec's introduction to Japanese art, and wine-bottles. In one corner, propped against the wall, was a stack of paintings including a *Seated Dancing-girl*, the *Portrait of the Actor Henry Samary* (page 75) in a mauve tail-coat, those of *The Policeman's Daughter* (page 92), the *Woman with Sunshade in a Garden*, *Hélène V*, a pretty slender girl (page 52), *A Woman at her Toilet* and a *Girl with the Kiss-curl*—not to mention portraits of Lily Granier, Gauzi, and several local washerwomen.

The year 1889 was decidedly an auspicious one, not so much because of the Exhibition, or even because of the success Lautrec won with his *Dance at the Moulin de la Galette* at the 'Salon des Indépendants', as because on 5th October of that year he discovered what was henceforth to be his best-stocked hunting-ground, the Moulin Rouge—the loveliest night-flower in Montmartre, the most brilliant, and most highly scented too, for it contained La Goulue, queen of the dance and of vice.

THE MOULIN ROUGE

Until this time, the hub of Montmartre night-life had lain eastward, where the Boulevard Barbès meets the rue Rochechouart. The nocturnal public of the *cafés-chantants* went no further west than the Place Pigalle; there were, indeed, cafés in the Place Clichy, but they were daytime ones. But now the first businessman to impinge on Paris entertainment began to rush westwards, thrusting back the frontiers of darkness. This was Joseph Oller. He was a Catalan, vaguely connected with painting through one of his cousins, Francisco Oller y Cestero, friend of Cézanne and Pissarro; but what interested him was not painting, it was business. He had already opened the Théâtre des Nouveautés, the Rochechouart swimming-baths, the New Circus, the 'Montagnes Russes' and the 'Pari Mutuel'. Now he went into partnership with Zidler, an Alsatian, and they bought a plot of land at 90 Boulevard de Clichy, where a dance-hall known as La Reine Blanche had formerly stood. Willette, regarded as the best scene-painter in Montmartre, designed the interior of the future establishment—a music-hall, of course—decorated its façade, and found a name for it: the Moulin Rouge. The plan was simple, comprising a

TWO WOMEN, c. 1891
São Paolo Museum

wide gallery, a frame-built main room, and a garden for the donkey-
rides which were such a popular feature.

The formal opening took place on 5th October and Paris society
attended; Oller and Zidler had sent out a thousand engraved invita-
tion-cards. This aristocracy of the gay life included Count de la
Rochefoucauld, Prince Troubetskoy, Elie de Talleyrand, the Prince
de Sagan, Aurélien Scholl, successful Salon painters such as Stevens
and Gervex, American and English journalists who were devotees

WOMAN AT HER WINDOW, 1893
Museum of Albi

of 'the halls', and writers. One of these, Henri Verdier, now completely forgotten, wrote an amusing novel entitled *La Vierge du Moulin
Rouge*, in which he describes the atmosphere of the place: 'A noisy
crowd was bobbing about in the bright haze of vapour and reddish
motes that rose as high as the chandeliers and the gilded bronze wall-
brackets, clouding the mirrors and picture-frames—already dulled by
cigar-smoke and the dust raised by the quadrilles ... The male
dancers went their own way, unconcerned with their partners, whose

skirts flew round with a frenzied swirl, allowing glimpses of thin, lacy petticoats and rosy, transparent skin. At the far end of the room, on a platform edged with footlights, the orchestra was performing with formidable impetuosity ... The deep voices of serious men could be heard through the reddish mist—"Higher, La Goulue—go on—higher!" ... Fat hands clapped the more and more revealing exhibition, particularly when one of the girls, secretly disgusted with this crowd which had paid to see her underwear and wanted its money's worth, slapped her bustle and shouted some vulgar word or insult for the benefit of all these hopeless swine.'

Lautrec was there, of course, with his friends the Greniers, Dr Bourges and Gabriel Tapié de Céleyran, a cousin he had met again during the last holidays and who had taken French leave from Lille University for this occasion. The occasion was important enough, for Lautrec's *Bare-back Rider at the Circus Fernando* hung in the entrance-hall, and La Goulue, Valentin le Désossé, Grille d'Egout, Rayon d'Or, Marie Casse Nez and Môme Fromage were there as well, Zidler having lured them away from the Elysée-Montmartre. The first night was a triumph for La Goulue; Yvette Guilbert described her act some years later: 'La Goulue, in her black silk stockings, caught her black-satin shod foot in one hand, gave a twirl to the sixty yards of lace on her petticoats, and revealed her drawers which were comically embroidered with a heart, stretching roguishly across her little bottom ; when she curtsied in pert salutation, her adorable legs—agile, witty, tantalizing legs—would appear for a moment, then vanish behind the big rosettes of pink ribbon at her knees and the enchanting foam of lace that fell to her ankles. She removed her partner's hat with a neat kick, and did the splits, with head and shoulders erect, her sky-blue satin blouse showing off her slender waist, and her black satin skirt, cut like an umbrella, spreading out in a circle more than five yards across. And it was magnificent. La Goulue was pretty, and looked witty, if vulgar. She was blonde, her hair cut in a fringe at the level of her eyebrows and piled on the top of her head like a helmet, rising from a coil twisted hard at the nape of her neck, so that it would not come down while she danced. Her

MLLE DIHAU AT THE PIANO
Museum of Albi

celebrated lovelocks hung in spirals from her temples to her ears; and from Paris to the New York Bowery by way of London and the brothels of Whitechapel, every tart of that day had the same hair style and wore the same coloured ribbon round her neck.'

Lautrec foresaw that the Moulin Rouge would be an inexhaustible source of material for him, and besides, there at least he felt at home. Everyone there knew him, liked him, respected him, and most important of all, left him in peace. He was a looker-on at the 'love market' of the dance-hall, where only professionals danced, but where anyone could come to try their luck. He even made a friend there, a man after his own heart — Maurice Guibert, who was the same age as himself, worked as agent for a champagne firm and was an esteemed familiar of the brothels and English-style bars that flourished round Saint-Lazare station and the Madeleine.

In January 1890, however, Lautrec tore himself away for a few weeks from the multicoloured beacon of the Moulin Rouge. Maurice Guibert, described by a contemporary journalist as 'knowing more about light ladies than any man in Paris', had persuaded him not merely to send five pictures—including the *Dance at the Moulin de la Galette*—to be shown with the Groupe des XX at Brussels, but to go there himself, taking the opportunity for a little 'tour' of the 'lower reaches of Flemish vice'. Guibert pointed that out there would be few French representatives at the banquet, for of the others who were showing, Cézanne never left Aix, Van Gogh was a patient at Saint-Paul-de-Mausole, the asylum at Saint-Rémy, and Renoir disliked travelling. Lautrec did not need much urging, and disregarding the advice of Bourges and of Adolphe Albert, his engraver friend, he took the train to Brussels with Guibert. The inaugural banquet took place on 18th January. Wine flowed freely, and tempers quickly became heated. The Belgian painter Henri de Groux began to attack Van Gogh, accusing him of hectoring, trying to provoke people, and being an ignoramus. At this Lautrec rose in protest, supported by Signac, and challenged de Groux to a duel. The combat had a ridiculous aspect, because de Groux, nicknamed 'the blister', was a dwarf. He appealed to Mauss, founder and president of the Groupe des XX, who made peace and induced de Groux to apologize. The latter, incidentally, resigned from the Group and ultimately sank from view as an unsuccesful painter and sponger in Paris. Lautrec again had a great success at Brussels, and Van Gogh sold a picture, for the only time in his life *(Red Vineyard)*. But Lautrec was greatly disappointed by the local beauties, whom he found too fat and sloppy. He consoled himself with the wines of Monsieur Picard, president of the Belgian bar, who was his host and whose portrait he painted.

Lautrec was fascinated by portrait painting, interested solely in faces, bodies and their movement, through which he expressed what he knew about the outside world and his own view of mankind. On his return to Paris he began a portrait of the Dihau family. These were good friends of his — two brothers, both musicians (one played the bassoon at the Opera) and a sister, Marie, who gave piano lessons. They were also friends of Degas, whom they admired and venerated, and they arranged a meeting between the two painters in their flat in the rue Frochot — which was hung with portraits of Marie, with whom Degas had been in love twenty years earlier. Lautrec was anxious for Degas's opinion, but Degas had no great wish to pursue the acquaintance, though he acknowledged that Lautrec had talent, and that it was akin to his own. This prompted him to say to Suzanne Valadon, who enjoyed making him jealous: 'He wears my clothes, but cut down to his size.'

Désiré Dihau reading his paper in Pére Forest's Garden and *Mlle Dihau at the Piano* (page 101) were shown, respectively, at the Cercle Volney and the Salon des Indépendants. They are admirable portraits, showing a friend's affection without the slightest tinge of cruelty. The latter sentiment found expression with prostitutes, if at all.

Lautrec was glad to get to the Moulin Rouge; and his studio took on an incredibly vivid atmosphere, its usually commonplace aspect transformed, when he began to work on his largest canvas, an interpretation of the dance. *'Je hais le mouvement qui déplace les lignes'* was a declaration that had no sense for him, to whom movement was very life. And he brings movement out by itself, right in the middle of *Dance at the Moulin Rouge* (page 78), where Valentin le Désossé

WOMAN WITH A BLACK FEATHER BOA, 1892
Louvre, Paris

AT THE RENAISSANCE: SARAH BERNHARDT IN 'PHÈDRE', 1893
Museum of Albi

prances in front of a red-stockinged girl who is dancing the *chahut* with a casual energy which suggests that this may be simply a rehearsal. 'Père' Forest's garden provided the setting for Lautrec's *Deaf Berthe*—who sits with her parasol across her knees and a foolish expression on her face, beneath the flower-trimmed hat — and his *Gabrielle the Dancer*, while plump-cheeked *Augusta* was painted indoors, in the rue Tourlaque.

At the end of May, Lautrec's friend Van Gogh returned from the world of the insane and settled at Auvers-sur-Oise, whence he later paid a short visit to Paris. Though in an extremely irritable condition, he lunched with Lautrec while there, on 6th July. Lautrec showed him the pictures he had on hand, which the older man liked and praised; but Van Gogh no longer felt the attraction of such beacons as the Moulin Rouge as in the old days. He was not 'up to the neck' in other people's lives, like Lautrec; he was infinite, devouring sadness. Three weeks later, at the end of his tether, realizing that this sadness would last for the rest of his life, he killed himself.

Oller bought *Dance at the Moulin Rouge* almost before the paint was dry, and hung it behind the bar. Champagne flowed in torrents under the sails of the Windmill. 'One may be ugly, but life's beautiful,' Lautrec confided to Lescau, the photographer. 'Let's carry on!' And on it all went, in a giddy round.

ART IN THE STREETS

'Lautrec really expressed himself best in engraving.'
GUSTAVE COQUIOT

Never had the walls of Paris displayed so many posters as during the
1889 Exhibition. Intensive advertising was needed, to induce provincial visitors to buy the manufactured articles now being thrown on the
market by a rapidly-expanding industrial system. Petroleum was just
coming into its own, for though electricity was supplanting gas as the
up-to-date method of lighting, oil lamps were still the most common,
and the invention of the 'Matador' burner, while it made them more
convenient to use, called for more refined paraffin. So there were
posters to sell Saxoleine, Luciline and other lamp-oils ending in *ine*,
posters to advertise bicycles—which had begun their career as sports
equipment and were now becoming the ideal means of transport —
posters proclaiming the merits of manufactured foodstuffs, such as
farinaceous foods, noodles, chocolate, the different apéritifs which
were coming into fashion, patent medicines (the makers of Géraudel
throat-lozenges may even be said to have given the first stimulus to
technical research on engraving for reproduction in the interests of
advertising), sewing-machines, furniture, cigarette-papers, even books
—not forgetting public entertainments, of course. Posters consequent-

107

LE MATIN: AT THE FOOT OF THE SCAFFOLD, 1893
Museum of Albi

ly adorned every wall and fence; they were ephemeral but exciting, and people were already beginning to collect them. Lautrec was enthusiastic about Bonnard's poster for *France champagne*, and put it up in his studio, side by side with Chéret's *Moulin Rouge*. He did not find the latter entirely satisfactory, but he liked its 'graceful lightness of touch', and it vividly suggested the different aspects of the place where he was now spending five hours a day.

For Lautrec, posters were an expression of life, a means of communicating with other people, and above all, an excellent method of collecting an audience. And he needed an audience—an approving one; he was no *peintre maudit*, glorying in doomed isolation. This is clear from the troubles he took to exhibit in every possible 'salon' and to join groups. But a poster designer needs orders, and to obtain orders he must show, at least once, what he can do. Here again, opportunity came to him from what he now regarded as his second home; Oller and Zidler asked him to do a *Moulin Rouge* poster for the opening of their third season, in 1890. This was no easy task. He had to outdo Chéret, whose poster for the opening had been acclaimed as a masterpiece. Lautrec decided to make a personification of the Moulin Rouge; instead of a general treatment he would symbolize dance by presenting the dancer—in his eyes there was only one — La Goulue. He already had hundreds of sketches and pastel studies of her; but now he must allow for the nature of poster work, its simple colour schemes and the way they could be combined. So he went back to his original design, made tracings, and produced from it an enchantment for the eye. Right in the centre is a highly-flying white petticoat, Valentin le Désossé is a greyish silhouette in the foreground, and the audience closes the scene behind, like a row of Chinese shadow-puppets. This brings out the colours — La Goulue's pink blouse and tawny hair — and the bright yellow touch added by the dress of an unseen dancer is like a kind of flower thrown to the queen of the *chahut* by one of her admirers.

This poster caused a revolution on the Paris walls. Printed in four colours, it was like a great shout of joy. As Jean Adhémar puts it: 'The flat tints, simple colour-scheme and bold silhouettes, and even

THE BED, c. 1892-1895
Louvre, Paris

Valentin's grimacing mask, reveal the ardent admirer of Japanese art;
but the whole effect has an originality and force never seen before.'
Lautrec's name—hard to decipher because of the superimposed H
and T — was now on the lips of everyone who had seen the poster;
but this, as the painter knew, meant only a temporary vogue. Nevertheless, it strengthened his conviction that this was the only kind of
painting for him—a vision of the world he lived in, transcribed in
bold, harsh lines, shedding the cold light of day on reality, carrying
analysis into the very heart of contemporary society, with all its fero-
city. Cormon's pupil had travelled far from the eclogues and pastoral
themes the master had suggested to him. Painting was no legend, to

PORTRAIT OF TAPIÉ DE CÉLEYRAN, 1894
Museum of Albi

his mind; it must take everyday life as its materials and transmute it. Constantin Guys had thought the same; but Lautrec unfortunately had no Baudelaire to sing his praises and force the public to regard him.

He had one friend, however, who was to fight valiantly for him— one he had just met again, after losing sight of him, at Boussod & Valadon's gallery, 19 Boulevard Montmartre. Lautrec had gone there to find out whether any of the pictures he had left with Theo Van Gogh had been sold. The friend in question was Maurice Joyant, who had been at school with him at the Lycée Fontanes.

Joyant was a man of good bourgeois family, who had some private means and was very much the dilettante. His appearance was distinguished, so were his moral qualities, and Boussod had asked him to follow Theo Van Gogh as manager of the little gallery. Theo had taken his brother Vincent's death very hard, and after leaving the gallery and receiving treatment for nervous depression from the celebrated Dr Blanche, he had died at an asylum in Utrecht In making the inventory of the gallery, Maurice Joyant had found several Lautrecs that Vincent Van Gogh had persuaded his brother to buy. They were stacked in the storeroom, together with pictures by Gauguin, Degas, Pissarro, Daumier and Monet—the last-named had a contract with the firm. In Boussod's opinion all these were hopeless propositions; but as he could not afford to lay out more funds, he left his manager completely free to arrange exhibitions and sales and even to take on new artists. In the course of time the existing list was lengthened by the names of Émile Bernard, Sérusier, Schuffenecker and Charles Morice—all those whom Léautaud and the *Mercure de France* were to champion so valiantly before long. But Maurice Joyant's entrance on the scene made no sensational change, and if Lautrec had not encouraged him with his unfailing optimism he would have been tempted to throw up the job.

As well as Maurice Joyant there had been another new arrival in Lautrec's life — his cousin, Gabriel Tapié de Céleyran. He was a curious personage. Paul Leclercq saw him a little later, when he was playing an active part in Lautrec's life. 'I was introduced,' he says, 'to Dr Tapié de Céleyran, whose tall, bent form, which seemed to have no shoulders, had struck me by its contrast with Lautrec's short stature. I was delighted to have this opportunity of meeting him and making sure that he was no myth, but really existed, in flesh and blood, that one could in fact touch him with a finger-tip without knocking him over like a lay figure or causing him to fade like a ghost. I scrutinized him. He had black hair, gleaming with pomade, which was parted down the back and carefully brushed upwards at each side. His whiskers were cut in the Austrian manner, leaving the chin bare. From among them, as though rising out of a fur rug, between his prominent cheekbones, there emerged a huge, red, pimply nose, on which gleamed a pair of gold pince-nez. He wore an old-fashioned frock-coat, resembling that of some ancestor in a family portrait, and when he smoked he drew slowly at his cigarette, as he might, at an earlier period, have taken a pinch from a great silver snuffbox, decorated with a massive coat of arms. His small, delicate hands were loaded with heavy, old-fashioned rings. Noticing, as we chatted, that my curiosity had been aroused by one of his extraordinary pieces of jewellery, he explained to me slowly and gravely that the stone on his tie was not, as I might suppose, a chrysoprase or an agate, but the tip of a sea-shell seven metres long; he told me its Latin name.

'I soon discovered that this serious old gentleman, addressed by everyone as "Doctor", was scarcely twenty-four years of age, that he had arrived a few weeks ago from Albi, and that in fact he was in his second year of medical studies. And I defy anybody who had the pleasure of meeting Lautrec's cousin about that time, to have forgotten the singular atmosphere the gentleman-doctor had built up around himself.'

It was not Albi that the Doctor had just left, but Lille, in order to complete his medical studies in Paris. He was now working under the celebrated Péan, the greatest surgeon of his day, a colossus from the Beauce region, the rugged, self-made son of a peasant family. Though rather exhibitionistic Péan was a genius at his work, operating on ovaries or stomach as another man would remove a mere appendix, and contributing enormously to the advancement of surgery.

JANE AVRIL LEAVING THE MOULIN ROUGE, 1892
Wadsworth Atheneum, Hartford, Connecticut

JANE AVRIL PUTTING ON HER GLOVES, 1892
The Courtauld Institute, London

Lautrec took firm hold of Gabriel, dragging him everywhere in his wake, snubbing him perpetually, forbidding him to talk about politics or painting, and using his name for the most atrocious puns; the one finally adopted, and used in introducing him to friends, was 'le Tapir de Ceylan.' 'Gabriel the well-beloved' took Lautrec to see Péan operate, and for days the painter watched the 'precision machine'. After the usual thirty preliminary drawings. Lautrec painted two or three pictures of Péan at work. The sight of blood did not worry him, he was immune from the weakness that descends on queasy minds at the thought of possible death. In his picture *The Tracheotomy*, Péan, with a napkin round his neck, looks more like a guest testing the tenderness of a leg of chicken with the tip of his knife, than a man carrying life in his hands.

The year 1891 closed with a triumph for Lautrec. An exhibition was being held in the rue Le Pelletier, in the gallery of a dealer called Le Barc de Boutteville. Among those showing were Anquetin, Émile Bernard, Maurice Denis and Bonnard. Lautrec joined them, not a whit disturbed by the firm's announcement of 'Impressionists and Symbolists'. The critics, on the whole, were favourable. Lautrec, interviewed, contented himself with saying modestly that he was working all alone in his corner and had no opinions on painting which were worth hearing.

His family had its opinion, however. This painting, it declared, was execrable and in the worst of taste; even his affectionate mother veiled her eyes. Henri was undeniably a 'bad lot', drinking, chasing women—and undesirable ones at that. As for his friend Guibert, he had painted him, in a bowler hat, with a girl who sat propped on her elbows at a table that was bare except for a bottle of rough red wine: and he had given the pair of them such expressions that one could feel vice steaming from the canvas like a miasma. All his drawings of La Goulue had piled up in the studio, with *Woman combing her Hair*, *Casque d'Or*, *Lady with the Gloves* and a number of portraits, including those of his photographer friend Lescau, of the younger Dihau brother, Désiré, and of the elder, Manuel. Never had Lautrec felt so free in his work, so self-confident. One night at the Moulin Rouge a woman took

THE HANGED MAN, 1892
Museum of Albi

a fancy to him; she was a redhead, of course, and rather enchanting, with almost yellow eyes which had earned her the nickname of 'the Panther'. There were a few feverish encounters, and then she went back to her protector. Lautrec went home and resumed work on the portrait of *Honorine P., (Lady with the Gloves)*. He was in love with her, but he never told her so. She belonged to a different world, 'the other side of the fence'. It is not only her hat which proclaims this; it is still more her face, full of intelligence and grace, with a touch of sadness.

JANE AVRIL

'One must be able to use the trivial to express the sublime, that is true power!'

J. F. MILLET

The year 1891 had been La Goulue's; the next was to be Jane Avril's. Lautrec needed a favourite theme to put him into a creative mood. He needed some particular woman to be the centre of his dreams of a haven where he would at last find appeasement and shelter from his stormy desires. If any woman had ever really given him her heart, Lautrec would most certainly have become another Degas, a placid grumbler, his horizon bounded by stove, easel and bed; for in his pursuit of one subject after another he was simply hoping to find a resting-place.

Jane Avril was twenty when she joined the quadrille at the Moulin Rouge; but before achieving what she regarded as success, she had passed through years of suffering which had left their mark. Her mother had been a Second Empire *demi-mondaine*—irascible, cruel and mentally unbalanced—and her father an Italian aristocrat. Her birth had of course been the result of a mistake, and the *demi-mondaine's* subsequent career proved unsuccessful. The little girl became the drudge and scapegoat of her mother, who beat her, terrorized

WOMAN IN A CORSET, 1893
Museum of Albi

THE KISS, 1892
Collection Mme Dortu, Le Vésinet

her, sent her out begging, and soon decided to put her on the streets
so that she should bring in money. She ran away from home and found
herself in the Salpêtrière Hospital, where she had treatment from
Professor Charcot before being restored to her mother, who henceforth left her more or less unmolested.

Jane Avril's vocation was dancing. She tried to earn her living, first
as a cashier in the rue du Caire and then at the 1889 Exhibition. She
spent her wages on dancing lessons and became a bare-back rider at
the Hippodrome in the Place de l'Alma, where Zidler saw her and
engaged her. In contrast to La Goulue, the embodiment of health and
vulgarity, Jane Avril was like a sickly flower. A pair of turquoise-
blue eyes lit up her delicate, peaky face and the slight pucker at the
corners of her mouth seemed trying to express all the world's misery
in a half-smile. Despite her hard life she was cultivated, fond of pictures, books and beautiful things. At the Moulin Rouge she was a

121

misfit, even in her style of dancing, and was not much liked by the other girls, who called her 'Crazy Jane'. She was dictatorial and insisted on choosing her own dresses and her own dance steps. Her lingerie was in mauve and orange muslin, her skirts were in mother-of-pearl colours or black.

Lautrec, a little tired of La Goulue's coarseness, was touched by Jane Avril's Pre-Raphaelite style. It also charmed Arthur Symons, a constant visitor to the Moulin Rouge at that time, who dedicated to her a poem he called *La Mélinite* (her stage name). Lautrec invited her to his studio to pose. She felt at ease there, poured out the tea, chatted, and created a curious but pleasant atmosphere. She was by no means an angel; she was being kept more or less officially by Arsène Houssaye, who was a trifle decrepit but rich, and she gave herself to Lautrec when he asked her, with the air of one ready to please an agreeable friend. However, she told him frankly she was not in love with him. This was a disappointment, but he made the best of it, and dealt with her much more gently than with other women, both in his picture of her leaving the dance-hall and in *Jane Avril dancing* (page 125).

Tired of the Moulin Rouge and her aggressive companions, Jane left, moving in turn to the 'Jardin de Paris', the 'Décadents' and the 'Divan Japonais' where she perhaps went a little too far in imitating the English dancer Kate Vaughan and her sideways wriggle of the hips which made her look like 'an orchid in delirium'. Lautrec followed her everywhere, faithfully applauding, and did three posters of her. Jane Avril was undoubtedly an influence in his life, and it may have been she who checked his natural tendency towards violent onslaughts on his subjects, in which he resembled Goya. It seems as though Lautrec was tempted to linger in this phase, where both his pencil and his brush have a caressing touch; and when he went back to the Moulin Rouge with a big canvas which includes La Goulue—combing her hair—La Macarona, Guibert, Edouard Dujardin and Tapié de Céleyran, all in the promenade, he produced something more serious, warmer in its general tone, and imbued with a greater gentleness than *Preparing for the Quadrille* (page 79), or than *La Goulue entering the Moulin Rouge* (page 82), with her cruelly flaccid breasts.

Lautrec had become successful. Once again the exhibition of the Groupe des XX at Brussels had brought him favourable notices, and so had the one at the Cercle Volney. From Toulouse had come a request for a poster to launch the new serial story in *La Dépêche de Toulouse*, of which Arthur Huc was then director. He went there to supervise the printing, for he would leave nothing to chance. This poster, *The Hanged Man* (page 117) — the story was about the Calas case — perhaps shows something of Daumier's influence, but more that of the Japanese with their flat tints. Writing later about this period, Jean Adhémar says: 'For years he had known Forain, and was a protégé of his father, of whom he did an excellent portrait. Degas was another of his masters. But in 1891 and 1892 their influence began to yield to that of the Japanese. He was very little acquainted with Japanese prints, but at Goupil's and Duret's he had been able to look through albums of work by Hokusai, Utamaro and Shunho, and their flat tints, bright colour and concise economy of line had captivated and fascinated him.

'He had obvious affinities with the Nabis, especially with Pierre Bonnard. It is hard to tell whether, as some people now consider, Bonnard's experiments came before Lautrec's, for they were working together for the same publishers and the same public, at the same time. Bonnard's *France Champagne* is said to belong to 1891, and so does *La Goulue*; in 1892 Bonnard did a lithograph for the cover of *Reine de Joie*, and Lautrec designed a poster advertising the book; in 1893 Lautrec did the cover for *L'Estampe originale*, which printed some excellent coloured lithographs by Bonnard, scenes of family life; and the latter also worked for *Escarmouche* and the *Revue Blanche*.' This was a productive period in which Lautrec was consolidating his technique. But he was also taking a keener and keener interest in 'character', in whatever was out of the ordinary; and this brings us to someone else of whom he became extremely fond — to Yvette Guilbert.

'Imagine, at the top of the rue des Martyrs, a little provincial café with a low ceiling, which when packed to the doors could hold between a hundred and fifty and two hundred people . . .' The little

JANE AVRIL AT THE JARDIN DE PARIS, 1893
Museum of Albi

JANE AVRIL DANCING, 1892
Louvre, Paris

café, thus described by Yvette Guilbert herself, was the Divan Japonais. The owner Jehan Sarrazin, had formerly peddled olives, going from café to café and selling them for five *sous* a dozen in a screw of paper with a poem written on it. When he had enough of this, he bought out a wine-merchant at 75 rue des Martyrs and did the place up in the latest fashion—for the Goncourts and the 1889 Exhibition had won new admirers for Japanese styles. 'The billiard table was painted blue and red and decorated with twigs of bamboo; little bells dangled from the gas-jets; the walls were hung with big silk panels . . .' Japanese or Chinese? It would be hard to tell, amid this eye-catching junk; but the waitresses and musicians wore kimonos, so the place lived up to its name. The Divan's other original feature was its singer. She too had first appeared at the Moulin Rouge and then at the Jardin de Paris, but with no great success. Perhaps those places were too big, for her thin, sharp voice did not carry very far. But she had one admirer, a former habitué of the Chat Noir and the Hydropathes—Maurice Donnay; and the partnership he proposed to her ultimately produced Yvette Guilbert.

She was a tall, thin young woman, with a skinny neck and skinny arms, made to look even thinner by elbow-length black gloves. Flat-chested, of course; and her face consisted of an immense mouth, a bulbous nose and a pair of black, hollow eyes. Her voice was acid, her hair was red . . . a red that cost her twenty-five francs a month, according to Jules Renard. Donnay realized that she ought to sing things specially written for her, and that love songs were not in her line. So from ten till eleven o'clock in the evening, she delivered her *Pièces acides*. We have her own records of *Le Fiacre* and *Madame Arthur*, but her first success, *Les Vierges*, is forgotten:

> *Ce sont des abricots pas mûrs,*
> *Elles ont peu de charmes mais ils sont durs*
> *Pour sûr!*
> *Les Vierges.*

These songs delighted Lautrec when he came to the Divan Japonais, for which the proprietor, who knew him well, had asked him to do a poster. But he did not take Yvette Guilbert as its centre of interest; he wanted to do the opposite of what he had done with La Goulue at the Moulin Rouge, and he planted Jane Avril in the foreground, with Edouard Dujardin, the music critic and founder of *La Revue wagnérienne*, bending over her. All we see of Yvette Guilbert is her dress and gloves in the background, the intervening space being occupied by the scrolls of the double-basses and the conductor's hands, as in a Degas. The composition is carried out in black, yellow and green, and it makes the most of what constituted the special charm of the Divan Japonais, the quality of its public.

But although Yvette Guilbert was kept in the background this time, she soon came to the fore, serving as the *raison d'être* of a celebrated album and a poster no later than 1894. As with La Goulue, Lautrec was waiting for the subject to ripen in his mind. His first impression was usually right, but it was not until his brain had analyzed the model's features and events had confirmed that first impression, that the work would flower.

'Posters are the only thing!' Lautrec said to Tapié de Céleyran, who was surprised at the time his cousin devoted to preliminary studies. The words show that Lautrec saw nothing inferior about poster art, with its simplified pattern, its intent to seize the attention and the imagination. And when Bruant, who had just been offered an engagement by Ducarre at the Ambassadeurs, asked for a poster in his turn, Lautrec was delighted and set to work at once.

As he knew, Ducarre did not want a design by him; he regarded him as an unknown beginnner, and preferred the well-filled, glossy posters usually seen on the hoardings. But Bruant, faithful to their years of friendship, did believe in Lautrec, and had insisted that the commission must go to him. The poster was exemplary in its restraint, with only one touch of colour, the red scarf thrown back over the huge black cloak. Its success was so tremendous that *La Vie Parisienne* had a slight attack of jealousy: 'Who will relieve us of Aristide Bruant's posters?' it protested. 'One cannot take a step nowadays without coming face to face with him. Monsieur Bruant is said to be an artist.

YVETTE GUILBERT, 1894
Museum of Albi

YVETTE GUILBERT TAKING A CURTAIN CALL, 1894
Museum of Albi

... How can he allow himself to be shown on house-walls side by side with the *Auer Burner* or the *Oriflamme?* He must be distressed by such neighbours.' But Bruant was not at all distressed, and thousands of people flocked to hear him at the Ambassadeurs. This was Montmartre's first defeat by the Champs-Elysées, the first sign of a new trend that the Butte was to fight step by step. The New Circus, which Oller had opened long before the Moulin Rouge, had not done very well at first. But now the public was besieging its entrance in the rue Saint-Honoré. The management invested in stage machinery which was considerable for that period, the ring was turned into an illuminated swimming-pool, and the new idol, Loie Fuller, had a fresh triumph when she came on there from the Folies-Bergère where she had been launched.

Loie Fuller, an American from Illinois, was another case for Lautrec. She was ugly. Jules Renard who saw her in a bus wrote: 'A common face, suggesting some fat girl with a mania for making up like an actress. Thick fingers with no joints, only her rings dividing them. An intermittent smile, as though the passengers in the bus were yet another audience. Vague, short-sighted eyes . . .' Yet when she danced she was transformed. Jean Lorrain saw her turning, turning, and 'swooning under the lights of a transformation scene'. Francis Jourdain was allowed to go with Rodin to watch her rehearse, and is more specific: 'Can this really be called dancing? Waving in either hand a wand she held straight out, and which stirred the thin material of her very full dress, Miss Fuller walked, hardly ever leaping, seldom running, but never allowing the upper part of her body to remain motionless. She explained that the special feature of her style consisted in this synchronization of the movements of her body with those of her muslin dress. And indeed her many imitators pinned all their faith on the magic of the projectors that coloured the waves, curves, shell shapes, spirals and flames into which their veils were tossed by movement, but which promptly vanished again. These others seemed to be favoured by chance, whereas Loie Fuller gave an impression of well-organized dynamism. It was only she who added to the fairy pageant that glimpse of the human form faintly shadowed through gauzy folds, which conveyed something of the thrill one associates with the Winged Victory.'

Lautrec too found that Loie Fuller had 'something of Samothrace' about her. This was enough to turn him to drawing her in half-movement, a portrait concerned only with the magic of veils and light. A note, no more! All commentary on the dance is absurd. Lautrec liked only to look at things, not to expound theories.

Jourdain also writes, very acutely: 'If no pictorial art is less symbolical than Lautrec's, it is because he was incapable of considering the life of a thing as distinct from and independent of the thing itself. No art was ever less allegorical than his, more free from 'obscurity and enigma. Lautrec thought with his eyes, he had no wish to dream...' 'To see and to put down' was his aim; he said so more than once to Maurice Joyant, whom he met every day and with whom he enjoyed talking about work. He had seen La Goulue so many times that he took her as the subject of one of the two lithographs Joyant commissioned from him on behalf of Boussod & Valadon. This was *La Goulue arm-in-arm with the Môme Fromage*, the other being *Englishman at the Moulin Rouge* (page 74). These lithographs are of exceptionally high quality, thanks partly to the drawing and partly to Père Cotelle, the old printer at the Ancourt Press, Faubourg Saint-Denis, who liked Lautrec and showed him all the tricks of the trade.

The engravings were issued in a limited edition, of course, and sold at twenty francs a print. Boussod & Valadon's clients had begun to 'nibble' at prints, Adolphe Albert and Charles Maurin being the first to specialize in this branch. In fact the nibbling was so pronounced that Joyant decided to hold an exhibition early in 1893, in the famous premises in the Boulevard Montmartre. It was not confined to lithographs, there were posters and paintings as well. As though nervous of showing alone, Lautrec asked Charles Maurin to exhibit with him. The Exhibition opened at the beginning of February, and the critics went to it. In those days the art critic was as influential as the theatre and music critics. Men like Roger Marx and Gustave Geffroy were regarded as authorities, and collectors were guided by their opinions when buying pictures. Now they published enthusiastic notices.

LOIE FULLER AT THE FOLIES-BERGÈRE, 1893
Museum of Albi

MONSIEUR, MADAME AND THE DOG, 1893
Museum of Albi

Roger Marx wrote that it was a long time since he had come across an artist of such talent. Geffroy declared that the personality emanating from this work was incomparable. On the painters' side, Degas praised Lautrec in public, but advised his friends to buy Maurin, in whom he saw a kind of Rembrandt, rather than Lautrec, whom he said was like Gavarni, the painter of a period. Lautrec never knew of this, and he kept his friendly feeling for the jealous Degas who said to him with hypocrisy, after visiting the exhibition: 'Well, Lautrec, that shows you belong to the fraternity!'

For Lautrec the wind was in the right quarter. Collectors were gradually beginning to consider him with respect. As usual, he had attracted attention at the annual show of the Groupe des XX in Brussels, which still kept going, thanks to Mauss. He was invited to Ixelles and Antwerp; but everyday life was always the same—namely, tedious. Dr Bourges had got married, and Lautrec had returned to live with his mother, who had taken a flat in the rue de Douai so that he should not be left alone. She obstinately refused to understand either the painter or his work. She showed an increasing tendency to regard his problems in terms of religion and bourgeois morality. She wanted him to marry and settle down, in other words to stop drinking too much, killing himself with work, and running after women who were willing to sleep with him because he paid them. But what woman of his own world would have him? Although Joyant relates that one of them said to him when Lautrec died: 'I would have been quite ready to take on Lautrec, I think I could have saved him by marrying him . . .' Can this have been Honorine P., whom he painted so lovingly? We shall never know; but Lautrec himself knew that the only women who showed a certain delicacy of feeling towards him, an affection that was feminine rather than purely maternal, and who were frank and straightforward with him, were the girls in the brothels.

BIG MIREILLE

'All that a man is good for is to love the fellow-creature he knows, comes in contact with, or possesses.'

THÉOPHILE GAUTIER

When Toulouse-Lautrec first decided to become a painter, Cardinal Bouret, Bishop of Rodez, said to him: 'My dear son, you could have chosen no finer career, but no more dangerous one.' Those were the words of a man so liberal as to be regarded as a Socialist even in his own part of France, which was that of Jaurès; but Lautrec had not believed them. For him the only danger lay in not becoming a great artist, in not risking his life and soul; and when another ecclesiastic, a friend of his mother, reproached him for not thinking of eternity, he had the audacity to reply 'Well, yes, Abbé; but don't worry, I'm digging my grave with my tail!'

Thus, Lautrec was never in the least disturbed by the fear of death, of the devil, or even of the morrow. He is the most perfect example of materialism, and of practical realism. He was comfortable in brothels, so why not live there? The first he had come across—2 rue de Steinkerque and 106 rue de la Chapelle—had not been very agreeable because the pace there was too feverish; but those in the rue Joubert and the rue d'Amboise were completely attuned to his need

135

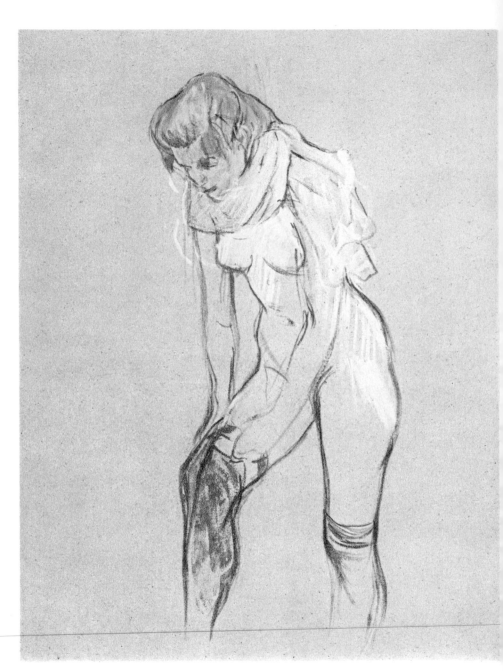

WOMAN PUTTING ON HER STOCKING, 1894
Museum of Albi

for peace and quiet. He was not the first painter to find inspiration in such places. Vermeer, of whom Proust was to write so well a few years later, Carpaccio and Caravaggio in Italy, Rops in Belgium and Baudelaire's friend Constantin Guys in France had all worked in them; so had Van Gogh, Emile Bernard, Raffaëlli and Louis Legrand —not to mention the hypocritical Degas, that shamefaced bourgeois. As for the Japanese whom Lautrec so much admired, they had spent their time there—partly because under the civilization of their country the geishas were the only educated women, and partly because they had models to their hand in the 'tea-houses'.

The establishment in the rue d'Amboise was a seventeenth-century mansion house, with magnificent Louis XV panelling, and the proprietress, Blanche d'Egmont (as she had been called in her *demi-mondaine* days), had better taste than many women in bourgeois society. She chose her girls carefully ; they were young, healty, and well-dressed—if 'dressed' is the right word—in frilly wrappers and amusing underwear. She collected pictures, and the rooms had period furniture and were skilfully lit. The place might in fact have been described in the words of Baudelaire's poem: '*Là tout n'est qu'ordre et beauté, Luxe, calme et volupté.*'

Lautrec was welcome here and settled down among the inmates; at meals he took one end of the table and 'Madame' the other. He went wherever he liked in the house, except when there were clients about; he sat in the salon playing endless games of faro, he wrote letters for girls who were unskilful with the pen, he listened to their confidences, stood them champagne, and comforted them in woeful moments. There was a school of literature at the time which described such women as cattle, dwelling heavily on the melancholy circumstances of these 'chattels'. But their circumstances were in reality a great deal easier than those of a charwoman or the mother of a large family, married to some drunken labourer and living in a shack on the '*fortifs*'—the belt of dismantled fortifications that surrounded Paris. Comparing one job with another, the brothel was better paid and no more tiring. When the 'young ladies' went out to visit friends, they no more carried the stamp of their profession than did the shopgirls who were overwork-

WOMAN RECLINING WITH ARMS RAISED, 1894
Museum of Albi

ed by Messrs Cognacq, Boucicaut, and others. The moralists protested
in the name of virtue and love; but love has little to do with work,
and society was the first to encourage a trade which it regarded as
protecting its own daughters and wives from the onslaughts of
'monsters'. 'They're no more whores than the wives of head clerks
in government departments!' Lautrec would protest if anyone treated

YVETTE GUILBERT'S BLACK GLOVES, 1894
Museum of Albi

him to a conspiratorial wink; and it was true. 'Madame' adopted 'Monsieur Henri', and when she asked him to decorate the walls of her big salon he was as proud as though the Opera had commissioned a curtain from him. He painted sixteen panels with sixteen medallions in which the inmates were portrayed — working with the assistance of a house-painter and a pupil of 'Pubis de Chabannes'.

One of the girls, Big Mireille, had taken a fancy to him. When work was over and the front door shut, she sometimes felt disinclined to go back to her own room and would come to lie down beside him instead. Taking him in her arms, she would murmur: 'You're my own little man, let's go to sleep!' What more could he have expected if he had married a woman of his own world?

It is agreeable to read Francis Jourdain on Lautrec; he is refreshingly downright, in contrast to some other writers who persist in regarding the painter's life as a form of systematic Freudian compensation: 'For his part, Lautrec cherished no illusions, and seemed in no way grieved to have been always denied them. What did he know of love? Was he ever secretly in love? Did he suffer through having to conceal an unconfessed love — or, on the contrary, at knowing nothing of a sentiment which to other men, as he could see, brought torment and joy? There can be no definite answers to these questions... And it is just as idle to wonder what course his sentimental life would have followed had he been less physically repulsive. Lautrec's attachment to brothels would take on a tragic aspect, would it not, if we were certain that it was merely the consequence of despair, the miserable consolation of an outcast, the refuge of a pariah? One can imagine how pathetically Dostoievski would have described that life of shame ; but we have no grounds for supposing that Lautrec would have seen such a tale as the true picture of his own fate.'

After the rue d'Amboise, Lautrec discovered the rue des Moulins, where a 'bordel de luxe' was opened in 1894—at No. 24 (now No. 6). The gossip of Paris soon made its reputation. It was sumptuously furnished, in every style from Gothic to Louis XVI, and stocked with treasures, including La Païva's bed and her silver-gilt bath, in which the girls would lie naked while champagne was poured over

PORTRAIT OF LOUIS PASCAL, 1893
Museum of Albi

them, to be afterwards lapped up eagerly by the clients. The parlour was Moorish, the bedrooms Chinese, medieval (for amateurs of torture), ducal or Napoleon III. The amorous activities of the couples occupying them were reflected and multiplied in mirrors that lined the walls and ceilings. The walls themselves were hung with satin, brocade or silk. Pictures, sculpture and ornaments were distributed according to the fancy of the decorator, who had spared no expense. The fees were high and the clientèle correspondingly select, and many ladies of the best society came to see how this 'Temple of Venus' was run. They showed no surprise at the figures that brushed past them in the corridors—girls in First Communion dresses, 'nuns', 'widows' in their weeds, nautch-girls, geishas in their kimonos, 'lion-tamers' in red jackets and black boots—but without breeches—carrying whips. They perhaps knew even better than the inmates to what strange whims their husbands or lovers were subject. 'The biggest whores are the women visitors!' said Lautrec. For he had just moved in, and was already on terms of warm friendship with Marcelle, Rolande, Lucie, Elsa and Gabrielle — and, of course, with Madame Baron and her daughter 'Popo'. Just as in the rue d'Amboise, he was know as 'Monsieur Henri', 'the Coffeepot' or 'Little Priapus'. He was a mixture of client, confidant and fancy man. The proprietress, Marie-Victoire Denis, was a charming woman; he used to take her to the Opera on gala nights.

In her flat in the rue de Douai, Countess Adèle prayed that God would enlighten her son, who was bringing such dishonour on the Lautrec family. Meanwhile the painter was combining this extremely comfortable and diverting life (he found it so diverting that one evening when he was at a party in the fashionable rue de la Faisanderie and his host asked whether he was enjoying himself, he replied: 'Divinely, my dear fellow, it's as good as a brothel . . .') with hard work, for he was painting as he had never done before, and the series of pictures he did of women in these brothels—about fifty, and many studies—ranks among his finest achievements.

The Salon at the rue des Moulins (page 148) is one of the largest of these pictures, despite the fact that when it was framed it was cut down, removing two girls embracing, at whom three out of the five seated women were originally looking (this was revealed by the framer himself—the father of Jacques Tati, creator of 'Monsieur Hulot's Holiday' and other celebrated films). It is perhaps the finest work of its year—1894—though some·people prefer *En haut de l'escalier de la rue des Moulins: on monte!* or *Nude: Red-headed Woman crouching*, peerless in its keen observation and sweep of line.

Francis Jourdain—constantly quoted because as Lautrec's personal friend he is an unrivalled source of evidence — wrote later of these pictures: 'In painting the *Salon* H.T.L. had no intention of shocking people, arousing their pity, or even "making them think". It is a very fine composition, the outcome of longer meditation than the others, and its outstanding style raises it far above the episodic painting or "slice of life". It does not belong to the slickly picturesque, rather childishly acidulous "naturalism" rendered fashionable under the disguise of blunt forthrightness by certain youthful followers of Zola and the Goncourts, or by the systematic pessimists of the Théâtre Libre team.'

Lautrec did not actually work on the spot, but took his sketches back to his studio in the rue Tourlaque. This explains the finished perfection of the pictures, their studied, unhasty composition, which shows that they were not painted impromptu. They do not record the fleeting glimpse of a scene, but are the outcome of a fully controlled intellectual exercise, aimed at producing a masterpiece. In *Card-game, These Ladies, Divan, Two Women waltzing, Femmes de Maison* — that wonderful back view of a nude woman standing between a bed and a clothed woman, in his acutely perceptive portrait of Rolande, Lautrec is holding his hand, controlling it, taming it, not allowing himself to be carried away by the swift pace of his drawings: he has second thoughts about a colour, he commands a subtle orchestra of tones, finally releasing only what has matured, the result of ripe reflection; he masters his temperament.

There is no doubt that to some extent Lautrec was being provocative! He was highly amused by the bourgeois dread of houses of ill-fame. He thought it a great joke to invite Durand-Ruel to visit him in

MARCELLE, 1894
Museum of Albi

TWO FRIENDS, 1894
Tate Gallery, London

the rue des Moulins when the dealer was about to arrange an exhibition of his lithographs. And he was quite right, for the dismay evinced by his visitor on finding himself in the Salon amid a bunch of lightly-clad ladies was well worth seeing. But it is equally true that he sought affection. Besides, the brothel was a kind of secret society, where one good turn deserved another, where the sense of complicity made it easier to confront the hostility of the world outside. And more simply, when Rolande — the successor to Big Mireille, who had gone off to South America—took him in her arms and they fell silent, all blustering muted in the tender night hours, he could forget his surroundings, conscious only of a great, comforting warmth.

THE OUTER WORLD

'To know what everybody knows, is to know nothing.'
RÉMY DE GOURMONT

In his desire to paint, or rather his frenzy for painting, Lautrec was spending such long days in his studio that he seemed indifferent to what was going on in the outer world; yet that world was in a state of effervescence. Edmond de Goncourt—an unusual type of observer, it is true, for he never left his ivory tower, despite his air of turning wide-open eyes on reality—was noting, day by day, events that should have interested Lautrec. On 1st January 1894 Raffaëlli, Roger Marx, Frantz Jourdain (Francis Jourdain's father) and Jean Lorrain called on Goncourt to offer their New Year wishes. Carrière told him about the picture he was painting of the Belleville theatre. Helleu came to make an etching of him, Robert de Montesquiou to rave about Sarah Bernhardt, and La Gaudara—who never painted anything except fashionable ladies—to talk of his admiration for Rembrandt. In the little world of which he was the centre, Goncourt pronounced judgment: 'Degas doesn't look a day older; on the contrary, he has grown stouter and developed the florid complexion of the successful man. When someone mentions the sale held the other day he is surprised into a slight nervous twitch, and declares

THE SALON AT THE RUE DES MOULINS, 1894
Museum of Albi

crossly that collectors are second-hand dealers in private business; he can hardly disguise his horror of sales, where the high prices his pictures fetch today may sag tomorrow.'

President Carnot was assassinated on 25th June. On 30th August Goncourt went to the New Circus: 'The darkness, and the circus all hung with black, and a horse from Erebus with a kind of Loie Fuller standing on his back, beneath electric flames of every colour, gleaming with the mauve of a dove's breast, the pink of sugared almonds, the green of moss in the moonlight, all this amid a tempest of muslins, a whirl of skirts, sometimes lit with a fiery sunset glow, sometimes pale as dawn.' On 2nd September, Octave Mirbeau called to speak of his contempt for the Pre-Raphaelites, Frantz Jourdain of his admiration for Monet. On 29th November Goncourt went to the Ibels exhibition at the Bodinière; afterwards he described his flat and lists his pictures—by Watteau, Fragonard, Gavarni; by Japanese artists including Utamaro and Hokusai; by Chardin, Raffaëli, Carrière, Blanche, Forain, La Gaudara and Chéret.

It seems quite incredible that Concourt should have been unacquainted with Lautrec, considering that he knew Ibels and Degas and that Gustave Geffroy and Roger Marx were friends of his; but when we remember that in 1894 Paris was in a ferment over the Dreyfus case (Dreyfus was cashiered on 5th January 1895) and that Goncourt does not once mention it in his diary, our astonishment is mitigated. A passage in the *Journal* for 22nd April 1895 sheds an even clearer light on him: 'The present-day critics are trying to make a great man out of him: no. Guys is a heavy draughtsman and the dirtiest colourist on earth. His only real value is as the painter of low-class prostitutes accosting in the street. He has rendered the animal provocativeness of such a woman's face, the brow half swallowed up by heavy waves of hair, the lasciviousness of her uncorsetted waist, the way she rolls her hips in walking, the way her up-caught skirt bulges out, the way her hands are thrust into the pockets of her little apron, the loose hat-strings round her chignon, the excitation induced by the sight of her back and the bare arms emerging from the sloppy dress she wears —all this in aqueous green tints like a watercolour of the Morgue.' Lautrec being the prostitutes' painter, one shrinks from the thought of what might have been said about him by this arbitrary and over-worldly man of letters, for whom grace, or even affectation, was the supreme virtue.

Spending his life at the *cafés-concerts*, Lautrec obtained a view of the world which, though perhaps slightly awry, was adequate. General Boulanger's movement, France's colonial conquests and the Panama scandal were taken as themes for songs. The working-class community was violently shaken when at Fourniers the soldiers called out to

SEATED NUDE, 1894
Museum of Albi

WOMAN WITH A TRAY, 1896

deal with striking miners fired on the crowd, killing nine people. Lautrec was not being escapist when he listened to Tapié de Céleyran's talk without answering a word; but he was absorbed in his work, and events in themselves—the tattle of the day, in fact—did not capture his attention. What was there to paint in them? Francis Jourdain writes: 'It would be vain to search Lautrec's paintings and drawings for any trace of these events, some of which were tragic, or of the agitation they caused. This is something extremely common, not to say constant, in art, which is generally affected only mediately, not immediately, by current happenings. The bonds connecting painting with topical circumstances undeniably exist, but they are tenuous; strong, perhaps, but often difficult to discern, and a picture can very seldom be chronologically placed on the strength of its subject.'

Goncourt may have paid no attention to Lautrec, but the anarchists' paper, *Le Père Peinard*, was loud in his praise: 'One chap who has the devil's own cheek is Lautrec: he puts on no airs, either in drawing or in colour. White, black and red, in big flat sweeps and simplified forms, that's his way. Nobody like him for spotting the face of a gaga capitalist at table with a trollop who knows the ropes and is giving him the eye to make him fork out. The only posters Lautrec has turned out are *La Goulue*, *Reine de Joie*, *Le Divan Japonais* and two for a fellow called Bruant who runs a grog-shop; but they have terrific swagger, aim and punch, and they take the wind right out of the sails of the fat-heads who want to be fed on nothing but pretty-pretty stuff.' Lautrec was not overjoyed by this praise; the anarchists could take themselves off as far as he was concerned. He did not blame them in the least for throwing bombs, and since 1892 they had been causing a stir. Ravachol had been guillotined and a number of bourgeois intellectuals had joined the movement; but it was outside his ken. He was more interested in the absurdities of Senator Bérenger's public decency campaign than in considerations of the nation's affairs.

Lautrec's world was always a restricted, or to be more exact, a professional one; and the great discovery he made between 1893 and 1895 was Whistler. After exhibiting successfully at the Salon, the American painter had settled in Paris, living in the rue du Bac, with a studio at 86 rue Notre-Dame des Champs. He was on terms of friendship with people so unlike one another as Boldini and Octave Mirbeau, Puvis de Chavannes and Aman-Jean, Robert de Montesquiou and Arsène Alexandre. Lautrec was attracted by his skill as a lithographer and his original views on engraving. The two men were experimenting along the same lines, both taking Japanese art as their starting point. They used to hold long discussions, after which Lautrec had made a number of successful designs, in particular his *Loie Fuller*, reproduced in the *Echo de Paris*. Another of his posters—for *Reine de Joie*, a bad novel by Victor Joze—had an enthusiastic notice in the *Revue Blanche*, which declared it to be 'bright, pretty, exquisitely perverse'.

FEMME DE MAISON, 1894
Museum of Albi

Faithful to his habits, Lautrec was now spending a great deal of time at the Jardin de Paris. This was a *café-concert* opened by the enterprising Oller in the Champs-Elysées, in what had been the premises of the 'Horloge' concert-hall; his clients came on there from the Moulin Rouge after eleven at night, in a special bus. In addition to the *café-concert* the place had a dance-floor, a bar, toboggans, booths where a fortune-teller could be consulted or a belly-dancer admired. The great attraction was Jane Avril. Lautrec designed a poster for her which had considerable success, being reproduced in three magazines, with favourable notices. There could be no better description of it than Jean Adhémar's, which runs as follows: 'Fair-haired Jane, wearing one of the simple dresses in elegant colours that she always preferred —a red and yellow one—over white petticoats, is waving one long, black-stockinged leg disdainfully, as though her thoughts were else-where; she looks tired and sad, one can hardly believe she is only twenty-six (Lautrec is thirty); her thin, delicate face is framed in the black ribbon of her big hat. In the foreground we see the long scroll of a cello, clutched in the hairy hand of a man with a strangely mis-shapen head.'

Whenever he found a particular line of work developing well, Lautrec exploited it to the full, working uninterruptedly. *L'Estampe Originale* having asked him for a volume on the *café-concert*, the intro-duction to be written by George Montorgueil, he decided to share the work with Henri Gabriel Ibels, a caricaturist of Dutch origin, and began to explore new places, such as the Petit Casino, the Scala, and the Ambassadeurs, where Bruant was still remembered.

Each partner produced eleven plates, Lautrec's subjects being Yvette Guilbert (the Sarah Bernhardt of the *'fortifs'*), Paula Brebion, Cau-dieux (the comedian at the Petit Casino), Ducarre, the pot-bellied director, whom he loathed, Edmée Lescot, the Spanish dancer, May Hamilton, an English *diseuse*, and Madame Abdala, who specialized in pulling faces. For this last he handled the lighting in the manner of Daumier, producing a nightmare effect. He enjoyed working with Ibels—praised so highly by Goncourt; he was cheerful, full of ideas, and good at securing commissions. The Ancourt Printing Press had never before seen so much of the pair. Georges Ondet, the music publisher, gave them songs to illustrate, so that Lautrec was able to make designs for his friend Dihau, who had written the music for Jean Goudezki's *Vieilles Histoires*. The quality of the songs did not matter to him; they might, as he said himself, be drivel, but he could have the fun of portraying Goudezki as a bear, led on a leash by Dihau—wearing a top-hat and carrying a bassoon—who is dragging him towards the Académie Française.

When he was in good form, Lautrec would arrive at Ancourt's works in the Faubourg Saint-Denis at five in the morning, by way of the narrow stairs at the far end of the courtyard, where there was a mixed smell of refuse and printer's ink. Lautrec was a craftsman by now, and very proud of the fact; he had picked up the craft here and there —from the Japanese, from Vallotton, the Swiss engraver who made woodcutting into a true art, from Maurin and from Adolphe Albert. He was devoted to Albert, and painted a loving portrait of his charming little wife, Renée Vert, who had a hat-shop in the Faubourg Montmartre. It was Albert who had him invited to join the *Peintres-Graveurs*, and he sent twelve items to their fifth exhibition. What he wanted was to make some more posters, but actors showed bad taste. Edmée Lescot refused, but Sescaut, the photographer, accepted; so did May Hamilton; then came two more for Bruant, one for Caudieux, and yet others.

Meanwhile, Lautrec was travelling about—to Brussels, Bordeaux and London. In London he met Oscar Wilde, and the well-meaning Whistler entertained him to a 'French style' luncheon at the Savoy. The lunch was an utter failure, and Lautrec consoled himself with whisky.

Painting—painting and drinking! Those were the only things Lautrec felt able and willing to do. He was sorry when *L'Escarmouche* ceased publication; it had printed a dozen of his drawings and lithographs, which were taken over by that astonishing figure Georges Darien for his anarchist paper. (Darien was the author of *Le Voleur*, a novel which had to wait for its success until 1956). To remain in the atmosphere, Lautrec began going to the Café Wéber, where he could

M. BOILEAU IN A CAFÉ, 1893
Cleveland Museum of Art, Ohio

THE MODISTE, 1900
Museum of Albi

meet journalists and writers on friendly terms and make himself better known among them. He used to take with him a singer about whom he had suddenly become enthusiastic—Cissy Loftus, an eighteen-year-old Scottish girl. It really seems that Lautrec, the solitary and individualist, enjoyed belonging to a group! And indeed he hated solitude above all things, and when he painted *Delaporte at the Jardin de Paris* or *M. Boileau in a Café* (page 156), he set them against a background of bustling figures, as though determined to bring them into his own particular universe of spangles and bright lights.

15th May 1894 was a red-letter day; it saw the opening at Toulouse, in the hall of the local newspaper, *La Dépêche*, of an exhibition arranged by one of the paper's directors, Arthur Huc, a great admirer of modern art. Seventeen artists had been brought together for the edification of the local population, who were conservative to the core. These included Louis Anquetin, Pierre Bonnard, Maurice Denis, Eugène Grasset, Ibels, Laugé, Maufra, Charles Maurin, Hermann Paul, Henri Rachou, Richard Ranft, Paul Ranson, K.X. Roussel, Paul Sérusier, Vallotton, Vuillard and, of course, Lautrec. Guidance was provided by a catalogue to which each had contributed a lithograph; but little notice was taken of the show, and where it was, Lautrec came off worst. 'No-one is a prophet . . .' said Lautrec to Achille Astre, who had come from Paris to write an article, 'but in any case they don't know what painting is about; they're the "Society for the preservation of the Provençal dialect!" '

This was not really said in bitterness. Lautrec knew exactly what he was about, and nothing could have induced him to depart from his own line.

NEW FACES

'The programme says "Scene design by Toulouse-Lautrec." I'd rather not stay!'

JEAN LORRAIN

It is possible that Lautrec first met the Natansons at Wéber's in the rue Royale, the meeting-place of the liberal 'intelligentsia'. Maurice Joyant used to bring rare pieces from his collection to show to good customers there, and with him came Lautrec, Tapié de Céleyran, and Guibert from whom the establishment bought its champagne. The Natansons were three brothers of Polish extraction who combined the business flair characteristic of their race with the lordly style displayed by many Slavs. They had taken very few years to gain a footing in Parisian society, and as their hospitality was lavish they were now surrounded by a small but fashionable court, comprising theatre people, writers, artists and politicians. Their magazine, the *Revue Blanche*, had been started to support Dreyfus and fight the anti-Semitic papers run by bourgeois reactionaries; but by this time it was fulfilling the same role that the founders of the *Nouvelle Revue Française* had in mind when they came on the scene about 1914.

Lautrec was fascinated by Thadée Natanson from the very first. He admired the man, who was tall, strong as an ox, and had an enormous

STUDY OF RIDER, 1895
Museum of Albi

appetite—but a fastidious one, for though a glutton he was unrivalled
as a gourmet. He also had an exuberant imagination, a caustic mind,
and an aristocratic indifference to bourgeois morality. Thadée Natanson had married a girl of fifteen, half-sister of the Polish sculptor
Cipa Godebsky and grand-daughter of a Russian prince. Missia Natanson combined great originality with great beauty. From one of her
relatives, a well-known Belgian musician, she had imbibed a love of
music, and she was an outstanding pianist. Money meant nothing to

THE REVUE BLANCHE. MISSIA NATANSON, 1895
Museum of Albi

her, beauty was the only thing that counted—as she showed by spending three hundred thousand gold francs on her marriage trousseau. She always dressed in light colours, and resembled some exquisite flower.

Toulouse-Lautrec was immediately attracted by Missia; she was certainly one of the strangest women he ever came across, and also one of the most varied. Her Memoirs are untrustworthy, since they naturally leave out her defects; but those who knew her, while unanimous in praise of her beauty, have little to say about her heart. Missia loved nobody but herself. When she married Edwards, of the *Matin*, she saw nothing in that distinctly shady individual except his money. She did not understand painting, or she would not have ended her days as the wife of J. M. Sert, a kind of Dali-esque decorator, who cut a figure in Spanish society as a 'man of the world' in somewhat the style of d'Annunzio. But Missia symbolizes an epoch and a circle recorded on canvas not by Lautrec, but by Vuillard.

The birdlike, whimsical Missia found Lautrec very ugly, but so intelligent, charming and droll that she adopted him at once as a familiar and kept him at her side like an affectionate clown. At least with him she was sure not to be bored, and besides he was wonderful at arranging parties, dinners and excursions to the most unlikely places.

Lautrec had found his ideal setting, and with it two new friends, Tristan Bernard and Romain Coolus. Tristan Bernard was two years younger than Lautrec; he had the breezy speech of the Franche-Comté and his thick black beard concealed a sensual mouth that was always laughing. Originally a lawyer, he had thrown law to the winds and was now writing short, humorous stories, editing a cycling paper —the *Journal des Vélocipédistes*—and contributing to the *Revue Blanche*. He earned most of his income as manager of the track at the Buffalo stadium, and Lautrec was soon infected by his enthusiasm for bicycle-racing, which he saw as a new and abundant source of material for drawings. Romain Coolus was older than the painter, but he was brought to heel in a few meetings and submitted with a good grace to Lautrec's caprices. The latter called him 'Colette' and led him forthwith to the rue des Moulins, declaring that he could write in peace and quiet there. It was a two-way process, however, for Coolus managed to drag Lautrec to the theatre. Another newcomer to the circle was Félix Fénéon, art-critic, inventor of the three-line news item, peaceful and phlegmatic anarchist. He had been dismissed from the Civil Service in this last capacity, though his trial, in company with the painter Maximilien Luce, on 12th August 1894, had ended in an acquittal. He was now editorial secretary of the *Revue Blanche*, to which he also contributed penetrating articles, signed F.F., on the work of his painter friends, Signac, Luce and Vuillard. His three-line news items went to the *Matin*, this being their style: 'Playing billiards on Saturday, Monsieur Duval, of Asnières, fell on his tail and put out his eye' (the French word *queue* means both 'tail' and billiard 'cue'). They were signed 'From our Special Correspondent', or 'By special cable', and Lautrec found them delightful.

He now had to conquer a circle very different from the *Caf' Conc'* environment where everything had been so easy. This needed a greater parade of wit and a less rough-and-ready approach. Yet Lautrec remained himself—with slightly more bitterness, perhaps, for he was enamoured of Missia and the fact was so obvious that he had to avoid being alone with her, since he would then be obliged to admit it and invite a rebuff.

In the whirl of novelty that marked the year 1894, Lautrec singled out one face he knew well already—that of Yvette Guilbert. He had never forgotten the impression she had made on him at the Divan Japonais, and for a long time he had been wondering how to approach her. Among the songs the music publisher Ondet had asked him to illustrate was Maurice Donnay's *Eros Vanné*, which Yvette Guilbert was then singing at the Scala. Lautrec made a drawing and the star sent him a note: '*Eros Vanné* wonderful. Am enraptured. Go on, young man, go on!' With this encouragement, Lautrec concentrated on her. He crystallised Yvette Guilbert into a type, just as La Goulue had typified the quadrille. He sent her a design for a poster, but she replied saying she had already commissioned one from Steinlen: 'We will do it later, but for heaven's sake don't make me so atrociously ugly; a little less! People who come to see me howl like savages when

COACHMAN TO A GOOD FAMILY, 1895
Museum of Albi

they see the coloured design.'

Is the design so ugly? The singer, a witty sparkle in her eye, stands with her face thrust forward, a tuft of hair crowning her forehead, her arms hanging down, her hands in their black gloves splayed out at right-angles like a duck's webbed feet. She seems to be in the act of singing a verse from one of her famous songs—*Les Vieux Messieurs*, *Le Jeune Homme triste*, or *Eros Vanné*:

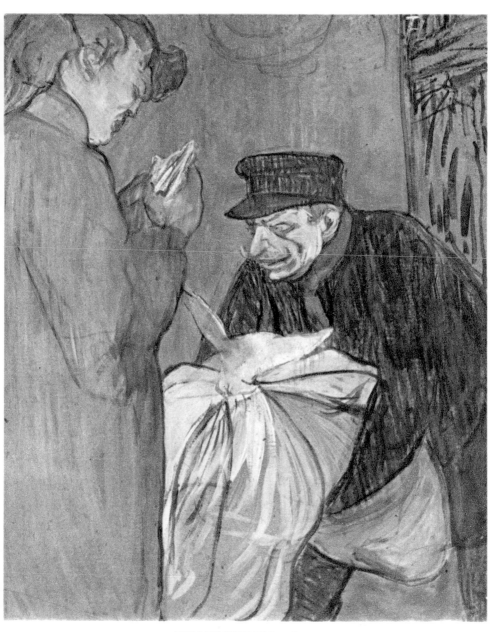

THE LAUNDRYMAN, 1894
Museum of Albi

Elles ne sont pas prolifiques
Mes unions évidemment
J'assiste aux amours saphiques
Des femmes qui n'ont point d'amants.

To help him make his point, Lautrec asked Maurice Donnay to take him to visit Yvette Guilbert. She was astonished when Donnay introduced him, and wrote many years later in her Memoirs: 'I saw a huge dark head, a florid, black-bearded face with a greasy, oily skin, a nose big enough to supply two faces, and what a mouth! A mouth that gashed the face from cheek to cheek, a terrible, obscene slit edged by lips that were hugely thick and moist, pinkish-mauve in colour. flattened and flaccid. At last I looked straight into Lautrec's eyes. What beautiful eyes they were—large, deep, full of warmth, astonishingly brilliant, luminous! I kept on gazing at them, and suddenly, noticing this, Lautrec took off his pince-nez. Aware of his one magnificent feature, he was offering it to me with unaffected generosity. His gesture called my attention to his comical little dwarf's hand, a completely square hand, attached to an extraordinary little puppet-like arm.'

Lautrec secured the singer's permission to come and work in her flat in the Avenue de Villiers. He was always squabbling with her, and displayed more cynicism than he really had in him, perhaps; but when he affronted her, her mobile features would flash into expressions that delighted him. She tried to bring him to reason, criticizing his life in the brothels; but he declared that the beauty of 'those women' was worthy of Gozzoli's brush. Lautrec adored Yvette Guilbert. Gustave Geffroy was to write the preface to the album he planned to devote to her, and one day that summer when they were all boating together, Yvette at the rudder, Lautrec remarked to Geffroy: 'How lucky I am to have been noticed by a star!'

When the volume came out—published by André Marty—Yvette was delighted and thanked Lautrec; but Jean Lorrain, the journalist, a jealous old 'queen' who always hated the painter, made a scene about it, telling Yvette she should never have let herself be painted 'in goose-shit' (the plates were printed in green ink). Yvette's mother agreed with him, but the volume of sixteen plates received excellent reviews—Clémenceau himself wrote an article on it in his paper, *La Justice*—so Yvette Guilbert duly signed the hundred copies that made up the edition. *La Vie Parisienne* wrote that 'This apotheosis of the *café-concert* star is quite out of the ordinary. The volume will not be forgotten, for it is unique of its kind.'

The plates were not all equally good, *Yvette en anglaise* and *Yvette Guilbert taking a Curtain Call* (page 129) being the best. But they enchanted a great amateur of modern art, who had just published a whole book on the unappreciated Daumier. This was Arsène Alexandre, who became director of *Le Rire* about this time, and asked Lautrec for a drawing of Yvette Guilbert. Lautrec produced it. It shows Yvette standing with crossed arms, singing her great English success, 'Linger longer Lucy, Linger longer Lou'. Alexandre published it, and it became popular at once.

Lautrec was now besieged with requests for work. He did a lithograph of the racing cyclist Zimmerman, who had just won the two thousand metres race at the Buffalo stadium. He made a poster for *L'Artisan Moderne*, and another to launch *Babylone d'Allemagne*, a novel on the vices of society. This latter was a tremendous success, and Sagot, the dealer, declared that after it appeared Lautrec's work had increased fourfold in value.

Meanwhile, the Montmartre Lautrec had loved so dearly was breaking up. The Elysée Montmartre had closed down, the Chat Noir was sold. Bruant, having made a fortune, had retired and bought the château at Courtenay, the village he had left as a penniless boy. He had even got married, to Mathilde Tarquini d'Or, a singer at the Opéra Comique, who championed her husband's bitter, beautiful works to the end of her life. The pleasure-world of Paris was moving to the foot of the Butte. The Moulin Rouge had been succeeded by a new 'beacon' — also belonging to Oller — the Olympia, on the Boulevard des Capucines. A new star was born: Polaire.

But did anyone still believe in stars? No more than Lautrec believed in love. 'But my little Yvette,' he once protested, 'men who are loved

PORTRAIT OF M. ROMAIN COOLUS, 1899
Museum of Albi

Que de Paimpol à Sébastopol erre
Le vieux monsieur, l'air pot, pot l'air,
Pourrait-il dégoter étoile plus... polaire?

POLAIRE, c. 1894-1895
Museum of Albi

by beautiful girls have nothing but vice in their eyes, vice on their lips, vice in their hands, the vice of the belly . . . The women too! Look what it does to their faces!' Yet he made some almost tender drawings of Polaire, the little Algerian girl with the small, sharp face. Polaire became the friend of Colette and her future husband Willy. Willy made the two young women dress alike and do their hair the same way. Colette described her singing: 'her whole body tense, quivering like a wasp on a flypaper, smiling with her mouth contorted as though she had just drunk the juice of an unripe lemon.' The same description applies to Lautrec's drawings of her; but he remembered her as the one who had liked and understood his drawing, when other people laughed at it.

THE THEATRICAL WORLD

In getting to know Romain Coolus Lautrec had made the acquaintance of the theatre proper, a change from the *cafés-concerts* with their one-man or one-woman performances. A new aspect of architecture was revealed to him now — the stage sloping towards the stalls, the boxes carried forward in a semicircle. His first pole of attraction was the Comédie Française, soon followed by the Œuvre. The first great actors he saw were Leloir and Marguerite Moréno in *Les Femmes Savantes*, and Barlet and Mounet-Sully in *Antigone*. He took a liking to Lugné Poe, introduced to him by Vuillard, and painted him in Björnson's *Beyond Human Power* and *L'Image*. He also painted Marthe Brandès, infinitely intelligent and already infinitely weary.

Marthe Brandès was just the kind of person to fascinate Lautrec. She was a musician, a painter and an actress, playing in the classics at the Théâtre Français and in modern comedy with Lucien Guitry; she already had a little court of writers, and Barbey d'Aurévilly used to present her with his books specially bound to match her dresses. Félicien Champsaur describes her as follows: 'She was dark-haired, her face a strange mask built up of broad planes, her eyes tawny and

BRANDÈS AND LE BARGY IN 'CABOTINS', 1894
Museum of Albi

feline, her mouth strong, with upturned corners, a red imperious hard mouth ... her figure was angular, but made graceful by her way of dressing, her voice seemed harsh at first but ended by charming the listener; her forehead was straight and high, the disquieting, haughty brow of a sphinx ...' This is how Lautrec sees her in three lithographs based on Pailleron's *Les Cabotins*, which are remarkable for strength unmixed with cruelty.

In 1895, Lautrec opened his theatrical year with a programme for the Théâtre de l'Œuvre, which was putting on an adaptation by Victor Barrucand of the Hindu play, *The Toy Cart*. Lautrec's design for the programme showed Fénéon seated on an elephant, blessing an invisible crowd from the heights of his howdah. Lautrec also painted the scenery, with the help of Valtat; but this was not enough to make the play a success. It flopped, and Francis Jourdain received no pay for walking on in it. The young painter followed Lautrec like a shadow, missing no opportunity for closer acquaintance with the effervescent life that attracted him.

An effervescent life it certainly was! Fénéon, the model for the programme, was a pleasant companion. Lautrec relished his strange anglicized appearance—he wore a check cape, bright red gloves, and a small bowler hat. Thus attired he cut a conspicuous figure, and the police, who had trailed him ever since his acquittal at the anarchists' trial, had no difficulty in picking him out at the increasingly fashionable Irish and American Bar in the rue Royale.

At the Wéber Lautrec was obliged to put up with some people he disliked, such as Jean de Tinan, Jean Lorrain and Willy, but there were others who amused him — Curnonsky, P. J. Toulet, Carlos de Castera, and Bracke, the Greek scholar, who was also the only Frenchman to have read Marx—and Charles, the *maître d'hôtel*, would steer them adroitly towards his table. At the Irish Bar, however, he reigned supreme, and would not allow anyone he disliked to be admitted. The place was a narrow passage with a single row of tables along the wall opposite the bar, packed to overflowing with an English clientèle—trainers, jockeys and racehorse owners. It was the English aspect that had attracted Lautrec, since Englishmen were not given to

RED-HAIRED WOMAN IN A PEIGNOIR, 1894
Museum of Albi

asking questions, and their impassivity tended to discourage un-
timely talk. The proprietor here was Achille, a Swiss from Vaud;
like the butler in some aristocratic household, he used to address his
customers by their titles. The favourite drinks were cocktails, which
owe their introduction into France largely to Lautrec; he declared
there could never be enough of them invented to quench his inexting-
uishable thirst. His companions, Maxime Dethomas, Joyant, Paul Leclercq and Ibels, could hardly restrain him; they themselves were heavy
drinkers, and their pipe-smoking—allowed here, though not next door
at the Wéber—made them thirsty from five o'clock onwards.

Lautrec was a goldmine for the bar. He brought customers, and two
of them—Footit and Chocolat, whom he had discovered at the New

ALFRED LA GUIGNE, 1894
National Gallery of Art, Washington, D.C.

Circus—even entertained the company. Footit had known better days in his father's circus in England; he had become a clown after losing at poker the horse he rode in his act at the Hippodrome. Chocolat was the negro in the pantomime they presented called *La Noce à Chocolat*, in which they were supported by an 'orchestra' comprising a banjo and a mandoline, played by a fair-haired Englishwoman and her mulatto son. At the Irish Bar they danced ecstatic ragtime numbers.

Eccentricity was frowned upon at the Wéber, and arguments were unpopular; they had to be concluded elsewhere. In his reminiscences Paul Leclercq tells of one that arose between André Rivoire, a poetical dramatist whose work had been seen at the Comédie Française, and Émile Voigt, the complete athlete (he even went in for deep-sea diving) about their relative prowess as runners. 'By about two o'clock in the morning, so many pints of pale ale had been drunk — to say nothing of Lautrec's glasses of port—that disputes on such subjects as muscle and wind were not unlikely to occur, particularly as the disputants were sitting down. But to settle the matter, Lautrec cried: "Let's test it!" And a few minutes later, André Rivoire and Émile Voigt, in their shirt-sleeves, were standing side by side in the Place de la Concorde, at the foot of the Obelisk. They were to run up the Champs-Elysées to the Arc de Triomphe. Lautrec was thrilled, uttering bird-like cries of excitement; he, his faithful cousin the doctor and a few other friends, followed the runners in two or three of the open cabs which used to ply for hire in Paris during the summer.

'Everything went smoothly as far as the rue de Berri, where the slope of the Champs-Elysées begins. And there we were obliged to haul the unhappy Rivoire into one of the cabs; he was limp as a rag and completely done up. Meanwhile, Voigt went on at a steady pace, breathing easily, till he reached the Arc de Triomphe.'

But the ideal companion for the Irish Bar was May Belfort, a dark-haired Irish girl with an exquisite complexion who had made her debut in London and then come to Paris, singing at the Eden Concert, the Jardin de Paris, the Olympia, and the Décadents in the rue Fontaine. She was a friend of Jane Avril and of another dancer, May Milton. Lautrec soon made a conquest of her, for behind a demure exterior she concealed a highly-developed taste for vice. She had an affair with Jane Avril, but was not, like May Milton, a declared and exclusive Lesbian. If a *micheton*—a casual contact who would pay for her favours—came along, she would take him. She was known to some people as 'the orchid' because of her pink, petal-like skin, and to others as 'the frog', because of her mouth. Lautrec was the antithesis of a *micheton*, and she soon slipped away from his embraces, but she still posed for him. Her act was an equivocal one. Dressed like one of Kate Greenaway's children, a white lace sunbonnet on her head, and holding a black kitten in her arms, she lisped in babyish tones:

> *I've got a little cat*
> *And I'm very fond of that,*
> *But Daddy wouldn't buy me a bow-wow...*

Her mixture of artificial childishness and *double entendre* produced a strange effect which delighted Lautrec, inspiring him to five brilliant lithographs and a poster. He did one for May Milton as well, and in allusion to the 'liaison' between the two he carried out the former in red and the latter in blue, 'so that the spots shall be married as well.' The May Belfort episode was soon over (her career did not last very long either), and Lautrec turned elsewhere in search of material.

He found it at the Théâtre des Variétés, which was then giving an operetta by Hervé, entitled *Chilpéric*—though for all its Merovingian hero it was no more Merovingian in style than Cormon's paintings. Hervé was among the best writers for the boulevard theatres and had Offenbach's flair for success. Coolus, dragged to the Variétés by Lautrec on twenty successive evenings, thought that this was perhaps not exactly good theatre and that his friend was going rather far; but the latter, seated in the front row of the stalls, towards the left, was wielding his pencil so heartily that Coolus said nothing. Lautrec was drawing Marcelle Lender, who had the prettiest back in Paris. In the role of Galswinthe she danced the fandango and the bolero with dazzling virtuosity. We may wonder how these Spanish dances reached Merovingia, but they were the great attraction of the piece.

MISS MAY BELFORT, 1895
Collection Leonard C. Hanna Jr., New York

Eew Ancourt, Paris

MAY BELFORT, 1895
Museum of Albi

This was not the first time Lautrec had seen Lender. She had made her debut at the Théâtre Montmartre, played at the Gymnase, and was celebrated for her style of dressing—*à la Robespierre*—outside the theatre. Lautrec had already painted a portrait of her, in 1893, when she came back from America, where she had been acting with Coquelin. This time he found her fascinating, he liked her rather prominent nose, her rather plump chin, the heavily made-up eyes which gave her the appearance of a girl from a brothel, her tawny hair, and above all her plump, well-turned shoulders. He immediately made five lithographs of her—one back view, one full face, two in profile, and one wearing town dress with a big bow of dark red ribbon at one side. Then, the German magazine *Pan* having become interested in his work, he did a head and shoulders of Lender which *Pan* printed in eight colours, a remarkable technical feat in those days.

When Lautrec was obsessed in this way with a particular sitter, he invariably proceeded in the same order, from drawings to lithographs and then to paintings. He had done this with La Goulue, with Jane Avril and with Rolande, and now he did it with Lender, taking a canvas of the same format (150 cm wide) for *Marcelle Lender dancing the Bolero in 'Chilpéric'* (page 185). His studio in the rue Tourlaque was turned upside down for this huge composition, where two shades of pink of equal intensity, one used for her petticoat, the other for her hat, balance the figure of Marcelle Lender, dancing in front of the toreador-tenor in his chalk-white stockings, the surrounding courtiers and the plaster arches of the scenery. The immense green floor-covering, its vanishing lines accentuating the depth of the stage to the left, cuts half across the canvas and vibrates like the trill of a violin beneath the soft chord of the pages' blue costumes. The artist's intention in this dazzling bravura piece was to show that, absorbed though he might be by the rapid art of lithography, he was still an all-round artist and could produce a masterpiece in five weeks.

Lautrec was short of time nowadays. He could not at one and the same moment be working, drinking, and organizing in Natanson's house, 60 Avenue du Bois de Boulogne, a private view of Vuillard's ten decorative panels that was to go down in Parisian history. Per-

MISS MAY BELFORT TAKING A BOW, 1895
Museum of Albi

ruchot describes this event, which took place one evening in February:
'When they came in, Natanson's guests—there were five hundred of
them in all—were not a little surprised to see the painter acting as
barman. For the occasion he had shaved the top of his head and all
his beard, except for two little "sideboards". Under his short white

linen jacket he wore a waistcoat made from the star-spangled material of an American flag. His assistant was Maxime Dethomas, whom he had chosen in preference to any other of his friends, not because of his skill in the art of mixing cocktails, but because of his gigantic stature; the two of them would make a ridiculous pair. Thus attired, with his clean-shaven cheeks, and with his assistant towering over him, Lautrec looked like an ugly puppet. His hairless face made his lips seem more swollen than ever, his mouth became a monstrous red projection. He bustled to and fro all night behind his bar with its load of glasses, bottles, blocks of ice, lemons, plates, sandwiches and salted almonds, brandishing his shaker, drawing endless recipes from the resources of his sardonic imagination, thinking up the most explosive mixtures, those best calculated to make the estimable company drunk. His intention was evident—what he wanted was to intoxicate the cream of the literary and artistic world, make the respectable lose their respectability, destroy dignity, tear off masks. He succeeded only too well!'

His victims were present or future celebrities—Alphonse Allais, Fénéon, Mallarmé, Vuillard, Lugné Poe, Bonnard—all the contributors to the *Revue Blanche* and most of its subscribers. As he waved his shaker, dreams of his impossible love for Missia whirled in his mind. Like Paolo Uccello, since he could not possess his love he painted her, just as he painted Polaire. But Polaire at least did not jeer at his art, and was in the seventh heaven when she saw herself in *Le Rire*, with head drawn down between her shoulders and arms dangling at her sides, wearing a wide, bell-shaped dress.

Lautrec dreamed of assembling all these women, transfigured by the footlights, like love letters tied together with a ribbon. He produced an album which shows them in succession—Loie Fuller, Sarah Bernhardt, Marcelle Lender, Jeanne Hading, Cléo de Mérode, Eve Lavallière, Jeanne Granier, and 'their men', those who acted with them: Coquelin, Guitry, Antoine, Mayer, Caudieux. Their features, sharpened in black-and-white reproduction, already contain the germs of their future decomposition. Talent and beauty, like love, must waste in decay, following 'the way of all flesh' to death and oblivion!

PREMATURE AUTUMN

From 1895 onwards, everything Lautrec had loved began to take on the hues of autumn. In his frenzied plunge into alcoholism, the painter had lost all impression of the fresh feelings that had prompted the rose-coloured touches in the canvases stacked in the rue Tourlaque studio. La Goulue, whom he had so much admired for her youth, her vivacity, her free tongue and her passion for the Môme Fromage, was now the mere shadow of her earlier self. Yet she had known tremendous success, she had been admired all over the world; as the mistress of princes and grand-dukes, who found her vulgar style amusing, she had made a great deal of money (her contract with Oller carried a salary of 3,750 gold francs a week), but she had quickly squandered it on riotous living. For a short time she owned a house at Montmartre, where she was continually at loggerheads with her neighbours, to whom she used abusive language and displayed her posterior.

She soon aged and grew stout, had to leave the quadrille and, having run through all her capital by this time, decided to open a booth at the Foire du Trône. The premature birth of a still-born child exhausted

CHOCOLAT DANCING IN THE BAR D'ACHILLE, 1896
Museum of Albi

MARCELLE LENDER DANCING THE BOLERO IN 'CHILPÉRIC', 1895
Collection Mr and Mrs John Hay Whitney, New York

her still further. She was now a fat, faded woman, bursting out of her tights. Taking a last backward glance at her past, she thought of Lautrec, always her enthusiastic admirer—though she had not returned his admiration and would never have posed for him if she had not been compelled to do so by Zidler. In a letter dated 6th April 1895, she asked him to paint something for her booth. He agreed, partly out of friendship and partly because he liked doing such things. He designed two panels, each measuring three square metres. In one he showed the dancer in her heyday at the Moulin Rouge, dancing with Valentin le Désossé in front of her usual audience—himself, Tapié, Guibert, Sescaut, Jane Avril and Fénéon, though the last-named had not been with them in those days.

In the other he showed her in her new dance, as an Egyptian Almah, with Oscar Wilde in the foreground. Lautrec had recently met Wilde in London, shortly before the trial which would make him an outcast from the puritanical society of Britain. By the time the panels were set up, the fair on its annual round of Paris had reached Neuilly. *La Vie Parisienne* described them as 'huge jokes by Toulouse-Lautrec, that immensely eccentric painter, who has been amusing himself with popular art, vulgar and dissolute. We see the *chahut* displayed in a fresco, we see the gigantic contortions of a symbolical public dance-hall! The colours are crude, the drawing incredible, but it is really amusing, and the artist has indulged in a strange touch of irony by putting Oscar Wilde in the foreground!' Was this a lack of understanding on the critic's part, or malice? Lautrec did not care. He had painted what he loved, the Montmartre that was fading away: Valentin le Désossé had retired, Nini-patte-en-l'air was giving dancing classes, La Macarona was in hospital. Péan had operated on her, but she would soon die. Others, of course, were on their way up. The female clown Cha-U-Kao, for instance: but it was not the same thing at all, although Valentin declared that this artiste was the only new-comer who came up to the old standard.

Autumnal hues! The visit to London had revealed them even more clearly. Joyant, wanting to meet Whistler, with whom he was doing business, took Lautrec with him. In London Lautrec found an old acquaintance, Charles Conder, who had returned there after four years of Paris: four years of knocking about between the Moulin Rouge and the Jardin de Paris, of half-finished paintings, of sketches and amusements. He was bored in his native city, although he belonged to the fringe of the group led by Oscar Wilde and Lord Alfred Douglas, whose lawsuit was filling the newspapers at the time of Lautrec's visit. For Conder, the arrival of his former crony was a pretext for long excursions to the British Museum, the melancholy pubs, to the shops, where Lautrec admired the charm of the delicate, sickly, fair-haired sales girls, or to the fish-market. Conder introduced Lautrec to Wilde, but the writer refused to sit for him. Lautrec's memory, however, had no difficulty in retaining the flabby cheeks, pallid complexion, small round mouth and dark-ringed eyes, and in addition to a striking, yellow-haired portrait, he did a lithograph of Wilde and a drawing for the *Revue Blanche*.

Lautrec certainly had no great liking for Wilde. It was not a question of morals, though the all-tolerant painter, as a virile man, was always slightly repelled by homosexuals; it was more a question of art. Lautrec, the realist, eagerly breathing in all that was human, with no taste for flowery language and no affectations, did not care for anything tortuous, suave or over-subtle. But neither did he care for a community that persecuted writers and interfered on moral grounds; he had himself been a victim of the deplorable Senator Bérenger and his vigilance league, which had one day insisted on having a picture of his, showing two women in bed together, removed from the window of Le Barc de Boutteville's shop.

The world was the same everywhere! But that was no reason for not travelling far and wide in it, and Lautrec seemed to be wearing seven-league boots on his short legs. He now went with Joyant to Brussels, where Octave Mauss had disbanded the Groupe des XX and revived an earlier Salon de la Libre Esthétique. He had always received a warm welcome in Belgium, and once again the miracle of good food and unstinting hospitality was repeated for his benefit. Luncheons at the Gigot de Mouton, visits to brothels and to art galleries. He waxed ecstatic over Cranach, but declared that the Belgian girls were really very ugly, too fat, and ate too much. Only the burgundy was of satisfying quality. The gin was too pungent, the beer too heavy. He returned to Paris, but left again on holiday. 'One doesn't go away enough!' he said to Dethomas and Guibert. 'Let's be off to Granville!'

PANEL FOR LA GOULUE'S BOOTH, 1895
Louvre, Paris

Indeed, the sea had always done him good. Disguised as a yachts-
man, with a flat cap and a blue pea-jacket with gold buttons, he explor-
ed the coast from Granville to Dinard. The stalwart Dethomas splashed
about in his striped bathing-suit—a ridiculous spectacle, no doubt, but
the delight he took in the water was touching. Rather than go back to
Paris by train and from there to Arcachon, where he was to join his

family, Lautrec persuaded Guibert to make the journey by sea. So the three friends went to Le Havre where they found a steamer bound for Africa, but coasting round France on her way. This was *Le Chili*. Not wishing to embark literally 'without biscuit' (a French nautical term for going unprepared), Lautrec had his own supplies brought on board; the staple item was olive oil, followed closely by liqueurs, burgundy and sherry. Garlic, onions, tomatoes and greenstuff were bought by the bushel and he watched every minute while they were being shipped. Lautrec's idea of a real holiday was to do the cooking himself, and until the boat reached Bordeaux he seldom left the cook's galley, except to renew the supply of sea-food. The delighted crew feasted from morning till night and drank till they could hardly see the riding-lights. Lautrec, in his lordly fashion, paid for everything. Money was never any consideration with him, and this also explains the uncompromising character of his pictures—he was not particularly interested in selling them.

At Bordeaux his desire was aroused by the sight of a passenger who until then had never left her cabin, No. 54. She was the wife of a consular official, going out to join her husband in Senegal, blonde and slim, with a coquettish face under her smart little Parisian boater. Lautrec decided not to leave the boat at Bordeaux. 'Let's go on,' he said, 'You never can tell!' Guibert indulged this whim, but decreed that the voyage must end at Lisbon. There were no developments, except in Lautrec's imagination. At Lisbon, Guibert flatly refused to go any further. Lautrec gave way, after an unsuccessful attempt to tickle his friend's fancy with 'the charm of fourteen-year-old negro girls'. They would simply go to Madrid, to take a turn in the red light districts of the town. But though Lautrec enjoyed dissipation, he was soon disgusted by the squalid prostitution he found here, its venality flaunted rather than disguised. The friends fled from Madrid to Toledo, where they discovered the Grecos. Barrès had not yet written about El Greco, and his work was little known in France. Lautrec was greatly struck by his barbarous yet ascetic vision, his fierce dashes of colour and the physical distortion which heightens the tragedy of his compositions ; but he remained quite uninfluenced.

PANEL FOR LA GOULUE'S BOOTH: DANCE AT THE MOULIN ROUGE, 1895
Louvre, Paris

Lautrec could 'catch' nothing from others; his work was his own.

Leaving Spain, Lautrec went back to Bordeaux for a fresh taste of the brothels in the rue de Pessac, before having himself driven to Malromé, where he could sleep and drink alone, under the shady trees, and dream of impossible loves. His family's utter failure to understand his work had ceased even to surprise him. He was unmoved to learn

LA GOULUE BEFORE THE BENCH, 1895
Museum of Albi

that nine or ten paintings he had left at Albi for safe-keeping had been burnt at the order of his uncle Charles, on the grounds that they were indecent. This incident—which was later denied by the family, and particularly by Mary Tapié de Céleyran—could have had no effect on Lautrec, for he was far from concerning himself with bourgeois reactions. At Albi his own father was considered to be 'cracked', but what did it matter? Life was rotten, but not unattractive. Everything that lives too long falls into corruption, summer is always too brief and autumn comes so soon . . . let us get to work!

Lautrec returned to Paris in September. Many things had happened during those feverish months, but he settled back into the old atmosphere, painting *Cha-U-Kao, the Female Clown* (page 197), with her muscular wrestler's chest rising out of a golden-yellow tutu, and his friend *Tristan Bernard at the Buffalo Stadium* (page 200). For once in a way, there is a corner of landscape here—the central enclosure and the stand—but it hardly counts in relation to the overbearing, thickset figure who is gazing at it with the expression of a sea-captain watching from the bridge of his vessel as the waves race by, carrying his life with them.

THE HEIGHT OF HIS POWERS

'Joys always come too late in life.'
EDMOND AND JULES DE GONCOURT

'Without recourse to phantasmagoria or nightmare, simply by re-
nouncing lies and determining to tell the whole truth, Lautrec has
created terrifying works, throwing the harshest light on one of the
hells of misery and vice that lurk behind our façade of civilization.
Never had shabby knavery, passive stupidity, bestial indifference and,
saddest of all, the fact that numbers of naïve-featured woman might
have led happy, regular, simple lives—never before had all this been
expressed so vividly, with such calm bitterness.' These lines, from an
article so forthright and well-constructed that it made the round of
the Paris art-world in a single day, were written by Gustave Geffroy,
the revered critic of the Académie Goncourt and champion of the
avant-garde. He had leapt into the fray in *Le Journal*, in defence of the
exhibition organized by Joyant at 9 rue Forest, in association with
a friend of his, Michel Mauzi, a lithographer, who also worked for
Boussod & Valadon.

This, in January 1896, was the most extraordinary show in all Paris.
Lautrec, with his keen sense of *mise en scène*, had assembled the most
daring paintings and the 'spiciest' lithographs of the exhibition in

IN THE WINGS AT THE FOLIES-BERGÈRE, 1896
Museum of Albi

GALA EVENING AT THE MOULIN ROUGE: ENTRY OF CHA-U-KAO, 1896
Museum of Albi

two small rooms on the first floor, which were hung with strawberry-red velvet and had green curtains and yellow furniture. This was one way of avoiding being closed down and prosecuted under the Bé-renger law; for these rooms were kept locked, and only friends and intelligent collectors were admitted. The first buyer who came forward was Isaac de Camondo, the banker. He already owned Manet's *Lola* and *Fife player*, Monet's *Cathedrals* and a *Dancer* by Degas. He chose *Cha-U-Kao, the Female Clown* and it cost him a thousand francs. This was the period when Vollard, who had set up as a picture-dealer in 1893, was selling Cézannes for between five and seven hundred francs. So Lautrec may be said to have scored a tremendous success. It did not go to his head, however, for he told several dealers who came to try out the ground that there was 'Nothing for sale'. This exhibition included some admirable paintings which testified to the artist's maturity, such as *May Belfort at the Décadents, Woman at her Toilet, Marcelle Lender dancing the Bolero in 'Chilpéric'* (page 185), *Tapié de Céleyran (page 111), Louis Pascal (page 141), The Card-players, The Friends, Mlle Pascal at the Piano*, and studies for an album on women in brothels, which did not appear until April.

This was an old notion to which he had returned after deciding against illustrating Edmond de Goncourt's *La Fille Elisa*, at Joyant's suggestion. For one thing Edmond de Goncourt was no friend of his. He had always snubbed him, despite the remonstrances of Geffroy and Roger Marx. And for another thing, *La Fille Elisa* was rather dated. So he did ten lithographs on daily life in a brothel. He showed the women washing, dressing, chatting, making love to one another, and sleeping in tranquil shamelessness. The album was published by Gustave Pellet, whom Lautrec had met long ago when visiting the Greniers at Villiers-sur-Morin. Pellet had just moved into a converted stable at 3 Quai Voltaire, where he was selling engravings by Legrand, Rops and Maurin. He was enthusiastic about Lautrec's work and paid for the publication himself. It was an album with a lithographed cover, entitled *Elles*, causing deliberate confusion by employing the same pronoun for the brothel inmates as for other women—whom Lautrec considered to be, with a few exceptions, no different from

CHA-U-KAO, THE FEMALE CLOWN, 1895
Louvre, Paris

the prostitutes who were his everyday companions in the rue des Moulins, or in the rue Laferrière where he was now equally at home. Jean Adhémar, who made a systematic study of Lautrec's engravings and is an indispensable authority on the subject, describes this album as follows: 'From the technical standpoint, the series is somewhat unusual: the ten plates were issued in a lithographed wrapper with no titles, no numbers and no indication of their order. It was the dealers of the year 1900 who gave each plate a number and a sort of caption. Moreover, five of the ten are in colour, the others either having a tinted background with the subject in green or old rose, or a white ground. In this, Lautrec was remembering Degas, the Japanese, and his friend Maurin; but he remains extraordinarily individual nevertheless. Among the best, one may mention *Le petit lever*, where a young woman in bed is receiving the visit of an older woman, in a white chemise. Lautrec must have been delighted by the fat shapelessness and ugliness of the women, for he was the first to make a fetish out of ugliness, as is so frequently done nowadays. *The Woman in a Corset* should also be mentioned. This shows clearly what nobility and distinction Lautrec could preserve, even in portraying such subjects. *Cha-U-Kao seated*, another of the plates, is justly celebrated. Indeed, it was the only plate that sold, for in spite of Pellet's efforts the album was a complete failure, and he was reduced to breaking up the set and selling it plate by plate to his very reluctant customers.'

The print-lovers of the period liked *Le Musèe Galant du XVIIIème siècle* much better than Lautrec's album. This was a volume of photogravure reproductions of frivolous works by such *petits maîtres* as Saint-Aubin and Moreau le jeune. In fact, pornographic titillation was more to their taste than the kind of realism used by Tristan Bernard in his *Mémoires d'un jeune homme rangé:* 'Lying on a rep-covered sofa, Daniel watched, as she moved about the room, a stoutish person who, but for the extreme simplicity of her attire, might have been taken for a diligent charwoman, so deft and expeditious was her handling of jugs and pails.'

Lautrec's chief aim was to see things clearly and express them, and it is a mistake to construe his vision as meaning that at the bottom of his heart he condemned the form of 'damnation' to which Baudelaire alludes in his *Femmes damnées*. When he went to the law courts in the same year, to make sketches at the Arton and Lebaudy trials, it was not with the intention of mocking the parliamentary system—for which, as a royalist, he cared not at all—but to collect faces such as those of Arton, the lordly vulgarian, and Mademoiselle Marsy, the sugar-manufacturer's mistress, nicknamed 'Little Sister of the Rich'. Arton, whose real name was Léopold Aaron, was a financier, a friend of Baron de Reinach. He had paid out one and a half million francs to members of the French parliament, as bribes to them to hush up the Panama Canal scandal. He fled abroad, was extradited, tried, and acquitted. Lebaudy was the son and heir of a manufacturing family from whom he inherited two hundred and fifteen million francs at the age of eighteen. In 1894 it was calculated—in print—that 'Little Sugar-basin', as he was called in allusion to the family business, could afford to spend three hundred thousand gold francs a day. He affected a love of art and lived in a big way — a present of a necklace to Liane de Pougy cost two hundred thousand francs. He had to go to law with his family, who wanted to give him a legal guardian. He won the case, was called up for his military service, deserted — more or less — and died of tuberculosis in 1895. This led to another lawsuit, where his mistress, Mademoiselle Marsy, was among the witnesses.

But to return to Lautrec's attitude. Francis Jourdain writes that: 'It would not be entirely vain to look beneath the skin of the nobleman —emancipated but not ostentatiously so—for traces of the anarchism to which so many intellectuals of his day were inclined. Some people have accused Lautrec, the aristocrat, of degradation. It would be more correct to say that this scion of a line of minor Provençal potentates, influenced willy-nilly by currents of thought about which he knew very little, had lost all sense of class, or rather of caste. Reduced to the democratic level by force of circumstances, he had become a bourgeois, a bourgeois too intelligent and too completely adjusted to retain the slightest arrogance. Because he did not despise the "vulgar herd" it was wrongly supposed that by the operation of some kind of sadistic feelings he was attracted to it!'

TRISTAN BERNARD AT THE BUFFALO STADIUM, 1895
Collection Mr and Mrs Philip Isles, New York

Lautrec was interested in contemporary life in all its manifestations. The event of the bicycle, for instance, was a phenomenon which had completely transformed life in France; the painter Ozenfant declared later that the bicycle had done more to advance pictorial art than the invention of Maroger's medium or of aniline colours.

In Lautrec's day reasonably priced bicycles had made exercise and country air available to the middle classes, and changing economic circumstances made these more numerous with every year. Bicycle manufacturers advertised both in the specialized press and by means of posters, which did more to promote sales. Noury Choubrac, Grun,

Grasset (for the Cycles Richard) were the first to vaunt the charms of the vehicle in this medium. Lautrec had been introduced to the joys of cycling by Tristan Bernard and had already done lithographs on Zimmerman, the two hundred metres champion. Now he made the acquaintance of Louis Bouglé, the French agent for Simpson bicycle-chains. Bouglé asked him to do a poster for Michael bicycles (Michael was an English cyclist who held the track record). The design was refused because the chain was not well drawn. Realizing that the purpose of the poster was to encourage sales, Lautrec was not offended. He tried again, and this time produced *La chaîne Simpson*, a poster portraying Bouglé and the racing cyclists Choppy and Michael.

MacOrlan tells us that Lautrec was enthralled by the colourful life of the cycle-racing fraternity: 'He loved the steep climbs, cornering at an angle of forty-five degrees, when the riders looked like glittering beetles climbing a wall. A hot, flag-waving, shouting, sensual crowd lined the track on either side, like a garland of human heads hung up behind the barriers over which the Gladiator firm jubilantly spread its name in huge letters. As a friend of Tristan Bernard, who was a genuine sports manager, Lautrec was made free of the cyclists' quarters. But what he enjoyed was not so much the race itself as the spectators' reactions. He painted or drew those who basked in the glow without being themselves leading lights. The six-day race at the Vélodrome d'Hiver brings them to life in an apotheosis of electricity and loud-speakers that undoubtedly gave them a new character.

'Lautrec was acquainted with the best-known "stayers" and sprinters, Zimmerman, Michael, Bouhours the small, fair-haired champion, Ellegaard from Denmark, Bourillon, Jacquelin, Contenet, Darragon. He knew the members of the famous *quadruplette* teams that coached the long-distance racers.

'The circling riders in their multicoloured jerseys provided an almost obsessive, almost tragic spectacle, as in every case when man achieves a precision of movement resembling that of a machine.

'Lautrec drew upon the strength of this throng without revealing the fact too clearly, for this sensitive, energetic little man controlled his impressions with remarkable intellectual acuity.'

MARCELLE LENDER, 1895
Museum of Albi

No subject was indifferent to Lautrec. Had he been asked to design a poster for the *Gyraldose*, which was then advertising intensively in the *Illustration*, he would have accepted it rather than one for *Bouillon Kub*, since it related to the intimacies of feminine toilette; but he had no definite scale of values. Other posters of this year include *Mlle Eglantine's Company*, for the troupe in which Jane Avril was dancing (the English critics found her too restrained), *The Passenger in Cabin 54* (in remembrance of the lady he had met on *Le Chili*) and *The Chap Book* (an advertisement for the Irish Bar in the rue Royale). With disconcerting ease Lautrec excelled in recording the day to day life in which he revelled.

He now turned to the world of Lesbianism. His first introduction may have come from Cha-U-Kao, for it was her he depicted waltzing

CLÉO DE MÉRODE, c. 1895
Museum of Albi

with another woman, the couple more than affectionately entwined. He had come across Lesbians in the brothels, he had been acquainted with the Môme Fromage, La Goulue's 'bit of sugar'; but the sight of them all together was an experience that was offered to him at La Souris, a bar in the rue Bréda, run by a woman called Palmyre. The most outstanding characteristic of those who met at La Souris was ugliness. The majority of them were stout, with a mannish build; their hair was cut short and they wore men's suits. The effeminate ones reeked of drugs and scent. The syrupy affection of the couples would have disgusted Lautrec, except that it gave him an opportunity of conveying in his drawings their insatiable desire for caresses. They willingly posed for him, for with them, again, he was the confidant. 'Monsieur Henri' was set apart from the world of normality, and they found it quite natural for him to watch them. *Abandon* (*The Friends*) (page 209) was the masterpiece prompted by his observation of Sapphic passion; yet it would be hard to find a painting more tender, more poetic, one might almost say 'more healthy'.

Perruchot mentions that Lautrec's output steadily declined from 1892 to 1899, and in 1896 there was indeed a definite slackening of pace; but the quality of his work was at its highest. *Maxime Dethomas at the Opera Ball* (page 212) shows incomparable vigour, and the contrasts of light (between the table, the glass, the hand and the tail-coat) have an affinity with Goya. *Woman at her Toilet*, the back view of a nude, is more powerful than a Rembrandt and the lines of its composition are 'modern' beyond their period. Lautrec was a poet of the flesh, who excelled in rendering the vibration of muscles shown up by lighting incidental to the surroundings. A woman is seated surrounded by her linen; her statuesque back contrasts with her scanty hair and with the cane furniture. (After a visit to the Van de Veldes at Brussels, who had done up their house in the Faubourg d'Uccle in 'art nouveau' style, Lautrec had hung the walls of his studio with Liberty prints and bought cane furniture, together with several green-painted garden tables.) She is clearly a 'flower of the asphalt', to use Bruant's phrase. Her thigh sags in a way that indicates fatigue. For all her grace, she will soon be forgotten. Even more splendid is *Model resting*, which

THE FRIENDS, 1894
Museum of Albi

may be regarded as a key picture. Here Lautrec renounces all trace of stigmatization and gives free reign to tender feelings, the charm of the breast with its rosy nipple, the sheen of a throat made for pleasure, soft stuffs, evanescent colours. The model—the same, no doubt, as in *Women at her Toilet*—is not named, but was very likely a girl from the rue des Moulins, Elsa la Viennoise, whom Lautrec used to invite to the rue Tourlaque; a lithograph dated 1897 shows her in a different style.

At the age of thirty-two, Lautrec had reached the culminating point of his powers of expression, had perhaps achieved all that he was capable of doing. Now practically saturated with alcohol, he was tense and irritable. He involved Joyant in a disagreeable incident by saying to ex-King Milan of Serbia, to whom Joyant was trying to sell a picture: 'After all, you are only an Obrenovich, a pig-breeder who didn't discover trousers until just lately.' Lautrec badly needed 'patching up'; but his visits to Arcachon ended in the brothels of Bordeaux, his spa cures in absinthe.

SOUVENIR, SOUVENIR, QUE ME VEUX-TU?

'The longer I go on, the more convinced I become that happiness is what counts and that it cannot be achieved in abnormality.'

ROGER MARTIN DU GARD

By the time he was thirty-three, Lautrec had behind him so many paintings, lithographs and drawings that it seemed as though he could regard his life as well filled. He could hardly find standing-room in his studio; he was still amassing the disparate objects that delighted him by their utter uselessness, and his sketches were bursting out of their portfolios. The canvases stacked facing the walls bore witness to the women who had sped through his life, contributing the gleam of a torso, the flash of tawny hair, the melancholy of flesh already tinged with the greenish hues of approaching decay; others were portraits of friends, and they were still faithful—Guibert, Dethomas, Tapié, Joyant, Tristan Bernard, Natanson. A kindly, familiar world, without fuss or problems. But can one really care for painted canvas?

In May of this year, when he moved to a new studio at 15 rue Frochot, Lautrec handed over eighty-seven pictures to the concierge of the rue Tourlaque house. Perruchot relates that 'these pictures met a lamentable fate. The concierge gave some thirty of them to Dr

PASSING FANCY, 1896
Musée des Augustins, Toulouse

ABANDON (THE FRIENDS), 1895
Private Collection, Zurich

Billard, the tenant who succeeded Lautrec. He parted with the rest
in the local taverns in exchange for a few glasses of wine. As for the
doctor's share, his servant began by taking the stretchers for fire-
wood, after which she used the canvases themselves as floor-cloths.
Having destroyed about twenty of them in this way, she realised that
the remainder would come in very useful to stop a few holes in her
cottage in Savoy, and applied them to that purpose. In the end just
one picture survived.'

Was Lautrec actuated by contempt for his work? By dread of these
reminders of a past that was too recent and too painful? Perhaps, more
simply, by lack of attachment to things, by carelessness, and most of
all by a feeling that the fun lay in painting, not in venerating the
finished output. Thus, he was able to revert to his favourite theme of

boxes at the theatre only by omitting all reference to his earlier paintings. He had certainly forgotten *La loge au macaron doré* when, early in 1897, he painted *A Box at the Theatre*. To annoy the respectable, he put into this box Tom, the Rothschilds' coachman, whom he used to met daily at the Irish Bar in the rue Royale, a girl from the rue des Moulins, and Madame Armande Brazier, proprietress of a brasserie, Le Hanneton, at 75 rue Pigalle. Madame Armande was a courtesan 'grown old in harness'; she was one-eyed, like Gambetta, but she kept that eye watchfully on her restaurant, where the clientèle rivalled that of La Souris. She was fond of no-one except Lautrec, for whom she consented to pose in the nude; according to Schaub-Koch the drawings that resulted were wonderful. In Lautrec's travesty of a universe, Madame Armande was the mother figure, evoking mingled affection and disgust. In this picture, which suggests some nightmare by Goya, she is glowering from under her hat at the play proceeding on the imaginary stage opposite which Lautrec has placed her. This painting prompted Lautrec to two coloured lithographs, published by Pellet—*La grande loge* and *La petite loge* (he did a third entitled *Idylle princière* in mocking allusion to a love-affair then causing much gossip in society, the Princess de Caraman-Chimay's passion for Rigo, a gypsy, who was not merely of low origin but ugly, with a swarthy, pockmarked face).

'Originally,' writes Adhémar, 'he had used theatrical boxes as an opportunity for scenic effects, their occupants being shown in the harsh glare of the footlights while the performance was going on. In 1897 the box provides him with an opportunity for showing, in formal surroundings and dress, figures who are seen in ordinary lighting, during the interval, with certain fixed attitudes and expressions; these are studies of faces and lines. *Female Clown at the Moulin Rouge* and *Elsa la Viennoise* (page 217) belong to the same group and they too are studies of colours and form. Pellet asked Lautrec not only for topical subjects, but for others which could be seen in retrospect: *Cha-U-Kao* was already ancient history for him, and now we find him making a lithograph from the *Two Friends*, a picture representing the Moulin Rouge, painted in 1894 (page 145). The great creative period is over; Lautrec is beginning to live on memories and regret.'

Perhaps to escape his memories, he now changed his residence, and to celebrate the event in proper style he sent out invitations for a house-warming party: 'Henri de Toulouse-Lautrec will be greatly honoured if you will take a cup of milk with him on Saturday, 15th May at about half-past three in the afternoon.' An accompanying drawing shows him dressed as a lion tamer, with spurs and whip, confronting a cow with bulging udders. Why milk? Because it had come into fashion since the dairy of the Domaine des Pins had opened at 54 rue Taitbout and Willette had captioned a drawing with a slogan proclaiming that 'A good cup of milk is better than a glass of wine'. Milk now being the drink of the snobs, Lautrec naturally caricatured the mode, for he hated snobbery. Needless to say, an account of the party appeared in *La Vie Parisienne*, which had always taken a great interest in Lautrec's doings, usually in order to make fun of them. 'Under the pretext of showing them his recent pictures and drawings, one of your youngest masters invited his friends this week to a cup of milk in his studio. A large "art nouveau" table held cups of milk, cream cheeses and strawberries... strawbottomed chairs surrounded the table, the walls were hung with mats, there were wild flowers in profusion... the very latest style of decoration... a smart barman in well-starched white jacket and trousers stood in a recess, discreetly preparing cocktails, to which the male guests, frock-coated and with flowers in their buttonholes, did honour, leaving the ladies to enjoy the picnic fare which was too spartan for them. The work they had come to see was almost forgotten, the courteous host having left it in the background. The guests were content to drink, laugh, flirt and gossip, while twisting in their fingers the lithograph sent out as an invitation, on which a handsome cow indicated the novel aspect of this summer entertainment.'

Paul Leclercq, who was present, gives a detailed description of the place: 'About a score of houses, each in its little garden, climbed along either side of this short avenue, which ended in a cul-de-sac. His studio was on the first floor of a small, square house right at the

MAXIME DETHOMAS AT THE OPERA BALL, 1896
National Gallery of Art, Washington, D.C.

far end. It was a high, bright room, cluttered with easels, tables standing in confusion, canvases, chairs, a training-boat (a rowing-machine) and a huge wicker armchair, in which he seated me when painting my portrait.

'A narrow, very steep interior staircase mounted one wall, connecting the studio with two small rooms, one of them his bedroom and the other his dressing-room.

'The place was simply furnished, but the dressing-room table held huge nail-files, nail-brushes of unexpected shapes and sizes, sponges of all dimensions, and many other objects whose use was difficult to discern at first glance. Little as he cared for appearances, Lautrec at one period of his life had had a mania for cleanliness. At that time he had bought here and there, as the fancy took him, every kind of novelty used in washing the person. According to him, the only soap that really washed properly was the kind used in the Turkish Baths. One of the attendants kept him supplied with this, and with the help of a short-handled broom he lathered his body with it, relishing its delicate scent of bitter almonds.'

To be a dandy! Lautrec often thought about that, and a dandy he would certainly have become if he had been differently constructed; but in his case the attempt was impossible, and he soon lost interest in the handsome brushes, and even in the charms of his bachelor dwelling.

Memories were difficult to escape. The syphilis he had caught from Red Rosa was progressing, and drink did not improve matters. Lautrec answered evasively when Dr Bourges, his one-time co-tenant in the rue Fontaine—who had just written a thesis on syphilis—advised him to go on a cruise. He agreed to a trip round the Baie de Somme with Joyant, and he went on a visit to Holland with Dethomas (travelling by boat along the canals), conscientiously admired the collection of Frans Hals at Haarlem, went to the Island of Walcheren to admire the butter-market at Middelburg as well, but did not see it. Then he returned in disgust.

He came back to drink in Paris, the only place he was really fond of, with Madame Armande, the Lesbians, Anquetin and Paul Leclercq,

AT THE BAR PICTON, RUE SCRIBE, 1896

Museum of Albi

CISSY LOFTUS, 1894

whose portrait he wanted to paint. The founder of the *Revue Blanche* agreed to sit for him, but did so for little more than three hours altogether, in numerous sessions broken off by the artist for visits to cafés. Lautrec seemed to be work-shy, which was a bad omen. When the Natansons invited him to their country house at Villeneuve-sur-Yonne for a rest he went, but spent his time stroking Missia's feet with the tip of his brush, as they both lay on the grass. Missia, whom he had once loved, had no inkling of Lautrec's sadness, or of his fears. For now he was afraid. In an attack of delirium tremens he had seen huge spiders in his room and had fired at them with a revolver, sobbing as he did so.

He returned to Paris for the theatre season and designed three programmes, one for a play by Frantz Jourdain, one for a Molière gala at the Théâtre Antoine, and one for Gémier's benefit performance. With a great effort he was finishing the pictures he had begun before the holidays—a nude study of a red-haired woman in a squatting position, which was yet another masterpiece, the portrait of Paul Leclercq, that of Henri Nocq (an engraver of medals and a friend of Marty; Nocq declared the portrait of him to be 'utterly malevolent': it is only fair to say that he was greatly influenced by his wife, who ran a drawing-school for ladies), the portrait of M. de Lauradour (a gentleman who was a friend of Joyant, with a picturesque turn of speech that delighted Lautrec, who once heard him describe Bruant as a '*tête de pipe bénie à l'eau de Javel*'), and that of Madame Berthe Bady (page 229).

For Vollard, who had taken over *L'Estampe Originale* from the publisher Marty, Lautrec did one of his last coloured lithographs, *The Governess-cart, or the Picnic*. Vollard gives the following description of Lautrec: 'I can still see Lautrec, that lame little fellow, looking at me with his extraordinarily innocent eyes and saying "I'll do you one of the brothel women". And in the end he did the "Trap" which now ranks among his masterpieces.' Vollard also relates in his memoirs how his servant told him one day that a strange little gentleman had called and would not give his name, but had picked up a stub of charcoal which was lying about and drawn his own silhouette on

ELSA LA VIENNOISE, 1897

the back of a Bonnard picture, by way of a visiting-card. After *The Governess-cart*, Lautrec designed a book-jacket for Tristan Bernard and one for Victor Joze (*La Tribu d'Isidore*—an anti-Semitic novel). Cover-designs for the *Revue Blanche* also prompted him to pull himself together and work seriously; but his hand seemed as though numbed by fathomless lethargy. His studio was tidy now, and there was no canvas on the easel. 'I was in a desert!' says Gauzi, who called on him there. Recalling the days when he had painted Yvette Guilbert, Lautrec began a drawing of her, but left it unfinished. He went back to the Irish Bar as though trying to recover his past, first the recent, then the more distant. A new year opened. His New Year card showed Madame Armande's dog surrounded by dead mice.

THE BLACK YEARS

'Happy, I thought, is he who attaches himself to nothing on this earth, but moves on in perpetual fervour amid the continual mobility of all things.'

ANDRÉ GIDE

The year 1898! Salis is dead, and Senator Bérenger too. 'Old Man Decency' has gone to the next world to join the man who introduced Lautrec to indecency in this one and gave him his taste for low haunts. Many of the painter's companions have died. Ervière has killed himself and so has Verdier, the landscape painter. Devigne, the Belgian sculptor, is in an asylum. But old Degas is still going strong—Degas, whom Lautrec still passionately admires, and whose opinion he seeks although he cares nothing for other people's. But Lautrec's first thought is for his pleasure, and that, alas, is drinking, more and more.

An English publisher, W. H. B. Sands, came to Paris to see him. Sands was full of admiration for the artist, and wanted to bring out an album on Yvette Guilbert. Lautrec readily agreed, for Yvette, famous now in America as well, was the figure of his personal mythology in whom he had remained most interested—and of whom he was fondest, too, although she perpetually criticized him. He did eight plates, much less caricatural than those in the former album, and now at last the singer expressed her satisfaction.

PORTRAIT OF CIPA GODEBSKY, 1896
Cleveland Museum of Art, Ohio

Lautrec was perhaps the most skilled lithographer of the period, familiar with the method in all its ins and outs; but by now it had become almost a routine, and he was bored with it. He produced *Woman at the Hanneton* (a girl wearing a hat, sitting in Madame Armande's restaurant with a dog) and *The Good Engraver* (a portrait of his friend Adolphe Albert, the aquafortist) (page 235), and then decided to try another medium, drypoint, on the advice of Henri Somm, a Montmartre artist who specialized in comic sketches. He bought some sheets of zinc at an ironmonger's in the rue des Martyrs and made some rather faltering experiments, followed by a series of quite successful portraits—Henri Somm, Tristan Bernard, Charles Maurin, Viscount de Brettes (an explorer), Sands (the English publisher), and Francis Jourdain. Charles Maurin showed him that light was more important than contrast in drypoint work, but—though Helleu and Bottini were using the medium with such grace—he soon gave it up. He was showing the first signs of lassitude in an inability to concentrate on one subject or medium for any length of time, a need for change of occupation and scene.

An opportunity for travel came when Joyant arranged a big exhibition for him in London at the Goupil Gallery, a branch of Boussod & Valadon—prompted to this by Countess Adèle, who was discreetly seeking for any possible means of getting her son away from Paris. It was agreed that Lautrec should see to the details himself, which meant his going to London well ahead of the opening date. He selected the pictures from those in his studio, asking his friends to look at them with him, sent them off, and then set out alone. The moment he had settled into the Charing Cross Hotel, he felt tedium in the atmosphere. He dared not drink for fear of becoming intoxicated and getting into trouble with the police, who were not pleasant to drunkards. He walked about London for hours, by himself; Perruchot tells us he used to go to the station to watch the arrival of the Calais train in the hope of seeing someone he knew. When Joyant arrived on 1st May—the private view was to take place on the following day— Lautrec greeted him as a rescuer. That was the end of his experience of loneliness and fear.

PHILIBERT, PONY OWNED BY E. CALMÈSE, 1898
Museum of Albi

NAPOLEON I ON HORSEBACK, 1895
Museum of Albi

The English public, of course, was the least likely of all to respond to Lautrec's frank, realistic, undissimulating art. The hypocritical society of the Victorian age inevitably disapproved of the daring scenes of women's life presented in these seventy-eight pictures. It also disapproved of the artist, who had not paid his respects in its drawing-rooms and was not sponsored by the Royal Academy. Yet the exhibition had been opened by a very distinguished figure, the Prince of Wales, the future King Edward VII—who had once been La Goulue's lover for a night. The story goes that Lautrec had fallen asleep in a chair while waiting for the opening hour, and that the Prince would not have him woken. 'Decent chap!' the painter is said to have commented. *The Art Journal*, the *Daily Chronicle* and the *Lady's Pictorial*, among other papers, severely criticized the show, and only one picture was sold—as another gallant gesture by the Prince of Wales.

Lautrec was glad to return to Paris again. He went to spend a few weeks with the Natansons and Vuillard painted him, in yellow trousers and a red shirt, with a scarf round his neck, cooking one of his dishes on their kitchen stove. This was a happy interval in a life that was growing darker with every passing day. Lautrec developed persecution mania and believed he was being trailed by the police. He would take refuge at 10 rue de la Fontaine Saint-Georges, where Edmond Calmèse had a livery stable; here the horses and the familiar smells recalled Le Bosc and his dreams of becoming a fine horseman.

The publisher Floury offered to bring out Jules Renard's *Histoires Naturelles*, if Lautrec would do the illustrations. This was something Lautrec had already thought of in 1895, when he met Renard at the *Revue Blanche*. He agreed, and set to work at the end of 1898, producing twenty-two plates and six culs-de-lampe. Never had an author and an illustrator been in greater harmony than in this book; but it proved unsuccessful and was remaindered.

The year 1899 began badly. A lithograph issued early in January, entitled *Conversation* and showing some Lesbians from the Hanneton, is so hesitant and blurred that one has difficulty in believing it to be by Lautrec. In February the signs of aberration grew worse, in a lithograph representing a parrot, a dog with pince-nez and a train. A

224

poster designed for Jane Avril, where she was shown with a cobra twined round her, could not be used at all. Lautrec was living in a mixture of delirium and panic, and in February he collapsed in the brothel in the rue des Moulins. He was taken back to his studio and committed to the care of Dr Bourges, who decided that the only course now possible was to send him to a nursing-home and try, as a beginning, to get the alcohol out of his system. With the reluctant consent of Countess Adèle, Joyant and Tapié, the painter, completely unconscious of his surroundings, was taken to a mental home run by Dr Sémelaigne, at 16 Avenue de Madrid.

A poor painter would have been sent automatically to the public asylum, Sainte-Anne. Lautrec was fortunate in that his family could afford to pay the fees of this establishment, the former Château Saint-James, which stood in grounds shaded by splendid trees and had retained its eighteenth-century furniture, with the additions required by modern methods of treating insanity. For many days he was tended there, gradually emerging from a kind of protracted nightmare to an awareness of what had happened and of where he was confined. Once he returned to his right mind his only idea was to escape from the place at once, so as not to die like a caged bird; and it occurred to him that if he could again become the painter he used to be and prove it by his drawing and his lucidity, the doctors would be bound to let him go. So he called his amazing memory to the rescue and did thirty-nine drawings on circus themes, using whatever materials came to hand— coloured crayons, Indian ink, pastel, red chalk and pencil.

Edouard Julien, the zealous curator of the Museum at Albi, who knows more about Lautrec than anyone else in France at the present day, mentions the outburst with which the Paris press greeted the news that the painter had been taken to an asylum. 'When he went to the Neuilly nursing-home for a few weeks' treatment, the newspapers spread the most shocking misstatements about the cause of his illness. "It was bound to end like this," wrote Alexandre Hepp in *Le Journal*. "Toulouse-Lautrec was making straight for a home. He has been shut up, and now madness, tearing off its mask, will place its official signature on the paintings, drawings and posters in which it has so long

STAGE-HANDS AT THE OPERA, 1896
Museum of Albi

GRAND CONCERT AT THE OPERA. AMBROISE THOMAS ATTENDING
A PERFORMANCE OF 'FRANÇOISE DE RIMINI', 1896
Museum of Albi

been anonymously present..." Then there was Lepelletier, in the *Echo de Paris:* "We are wrong to pity Lautrec, he is rather to be envied ...The only place where happiness is to be found nowadays is a padded cell in a lunatic asylum... After struggling, like most of mankind, amid the trials of half-madness, he deserved to enjoy, at long last, the divine nothingness of full madness..." It should be mentioned in passing that at this very moment Lautrec was producing, entirely from memory, his admirable sequence of circus drawings!'

Every care was taken to conceal from Lautrec what was being written about him. He was already afraid of being equated with other patients–such as the maniac who used to steal hats, fill them with filth, and hide them in the grounds. Joyant and Dethomas came to see him, but they did not bring the *Echo de Paris*, where Lepelletier's article went on in the same strain: 'He pursued love through thick and thin. In his unappeased pursuit he seemed to be expiating the too successful debauchery of the Counts of Toulouse; his perpetual defeats redeemed, as it were, their frequent victories in love. He was tortured by this desire to be loved, to inspire passionate affection. He was a hunchbacked Don Juan pursuing an ideal amid the most vulgar realities. He too could no doubt display his amorous list of the "*mille e tre*", but those thousand-and-three women's names could also be found in the lists initialled by Monsieur Will at the Préfecture de Police.' Poor Lepelletier! He was by nature incapable of understanding Lautrec; but he was quite capable of doing harm. So Lautrec's friends appealed to Arsène Alexandre, art critic of the *Figaro*. He came to visit Lautrec, and on 30th March he published a reassuring article entitled *A Cure*, in which he declared: 'I have just seen a madman who is full of wisdom, a drunkard who has stopped drinking, a man described as done for, but who never looked better... This "doomed" man has such intense vitality, this so-called abortion possesses such reserves of strength, that those who watched him plunging to his ruin discover to their amazement that he is now a new man.'

Two mental specialists, Dr Dupré and Dr Séglos, paid him a brief visit, agreed that this was no raving lunatic, but advised that he should remain under treatment, with permission to go out now and then. He

PORTRAIT OF BERTHE BADY, 1897
Museum of Albi

remained at the nursing-home until 20th May, the circus drawings being the fruit of his two months' confinement. As he put them away in a portfolio (twenty-two of them were published only in 1905, and the remaining seventeen not until 1931), Lautrec prepared to enjoy life again. He was free once more, except for Monsieur Viaud, the 'bear-leader' who was to prevent him from drinking.

Monsieur Viaud was an affable gentleman from Bordeaux, who had seen better days; he now had no money and no ties. He took on the functions of 'companion' and exercised them with considerable tact and intelligence, understanding when to allow Lautrec a longed-for drink and when to oppose his wishes, and keeping his protégé in a normal condition. Francis Jourdain tells us that 'The sick man and his bear-leader tacitly agreed in playing their pathetic comedy, though they knew it deceived nobody. Lautrec did not seem embarrassed by this enforced intimacy. He would present the newcomer to his old cronies as "My friend Messieu Viaud". Messieu Viaud would bow, shake the extended hand and murmur "Delighted..." In fact his task was a rather delicate one, for the essential thing was not to disturb Lautrec's illusion of having regained his freedom. If Monsieur Viaud was too severe, if he followed his instructions to the letter, he would make himself disliked and embitter the life of his convalescent charge, whom it would be prudent, tactful, indeed essential not to exasperate and who should be encouraged in his illusions—to which, after all, he himself might be clinging ...When I met them in the rue Notre-Dame-de-Lorette, Lautrec had not long been let out on remand, as it were. Neither in his appearance or in his mood was there the least hint of the trials he had just been through. He referred to them without embarrassment or bitterness... Lautrec's sojourn among the "loonies" seemed to have left no imprint of melancholy.'

Life resumed its course. Lautrec paid several visits to the Dihau family, went to stay at Le Crotoy for a time, and returned to Le Havre with the intention of embarking for Bordeaux. At Le Havre he took a fancy to a tavern, the Star, which had been adopted by the English sailors who put in there. 'Miss Dolly', the cheerful, fair-haired barmaid, reawakened Lautrec's desire to paint, and he wrote to Joyant (whom the Lautrec family had appointed as his guardian and trustee) for colours and brushes. With these he painted one of the finest portraits of his life, *Englishwoman at the Star, Le Havre* (page 237), and sent it to Joyant, informing him that he liked the place and intended to stay for a time at the Hôtel de l'Amirauté, with Lucien Guitry and Marthe Brandès. He remained on the coast until July, then left at last for Taussat, staying with Monsieur Fabre at the Villa Bagatelle, sailing, fishing and swimming. He did not paint, but when he returned to Paris he seemed to be in the pink of health and determined to work.

Lautrec's pictures were now fetching top prices at sales, the scandal associated with his name had died down, and on the days when he borrowed the little trap from his friend Calmèse and drove to the Bois or to the races, he may perhaps have genuinely believed that a new life was opening before him. Was it this sense of a fresh beginning that prompted him to make lithographs—as in his early days he had made drawings—of the world revealed to him by Le Bosc and by Princeteau, the world of horses and race-courses? However that may be, *The Jockey* (page 253), *Lady riding and her Dog*, and *Trainer and Jockey* were unquestionably successful, and the publisher, Pierrefort, was very pleased with them. With *In a Private Room at the Rat Mort* (page 241) (Lucy Jourdain, a well known *demi-mondaine* at supper Lautrec seemed to be turning towards different technical methods, and to be adopting a new way of looking at things. Colour was more important than before, whereas line was less clear-cut. If one could ever speak of an impressionist influence in relation to Lautrec, this is the picture where it might chiefly be sought! A touch of Renoir's grace in the model's smile is enhanced by the sheen of light on the mantilla; her arm rests on the table in a graceful pose well set off by the rather severe black of her supper partner's evening dress; he is seated in a very dignified attitude, his face hidden. This is not the work of an insane or physically incapacitated man; at no time is there any apparent connection between Lautrec's painting and his mis-shapen body. The lame dwarf painted like a giant, the drunkard's pencil never lost its startling lucidity or its terrifying analytical power; and everyone recognized him, though without perhaps admitting it, as the Saint-Simon of the age.

231

MLLE LUCIE BELLANGER, 1896
Museum of Albi

THE TURN OF THE CENTURY

'The ancient sages had all based their precepts on a strength of character which they posited without obtaining it; he alone had founded his ethics on the weakness of the human condition.'

JEAN PRÉVOST *Montaigne*

Amid the insistent rhythm of blue and pink waltzes, the smell of horse-dung on rain-soaked boulevards, the mingled light of gas and electricity, the twentieth century broke over Paris, which was living its finest hour—or so it believed. The *grands boulevards* glittered with the lights of the big cafés, the theatres and the luxury shops, but the outskirts of the city had never been so sordid. The wealthy dropped their gold by handfuls into the silken laps of the *demi-mondaines* or squandered it on race-horses and splendid town houses: but the earliest trade unions were agitating for a minimum wage of five francs a day. Hopeless poverty drove numbers of pretty girls into the houses where Lautrec slept at night; he was seeking consolation, they an escape from the slums of their childhood and the exploitation which was their lot if they worked in the multiple stores owned by Messieurs Boucicaut, Cognacq and others.

The World Exhibition was a triumph for militant capitalism, though it claimed to represent social progress; but the fruit was worm-eaten,

SLEEP, 1896

and only fifteen years lay between that display of smug optimism and the days when the bourgeoisie, smitten by the fear of death, would use their diplomatic wiles to send the working class to the front, lest one day they be smothered by it.

Lautrec uttered no criticism to suggest that he was conscious of this hypocritical atmosphere. In social matters he made no claims, merely remarking to the Cabinet Minister to whom Joyant had dragged him so that he should be given the Légion d'Honneur, 'Have you never thought, *Monsieur le ministre*, how strange I should look with the rib-

234

THE GOOD ENGRAVER: ADOLPHE ALBERT, 1898
Museum of Albi

bon in my buttonhole when I go to a brothel to paint?' When Joyant introduced him to fashionable ladies who wanted their portraits painted, he teased them, saying that the girls in the brothels had better figures and were not so spoilt. Speaking of his father, who was growing more and more eccentric and wasting his capital, Lautrec protested: 'And I'm the one they put under a trustee!' And when Marcel Proust tried to make out that aristocratic eccentricities had aesthetic value, Lautrec retorted, according to Perruchot, 'Typical bourgeois stupidity, always ready to gush about a ridiculous gesture or a sunset!'

Detached from the world and the age, Lautrec the painter continued his daily round, sleeping in the brothel in the rue des Moulins, filling his hollow walking-stick with brandy or rum each morning, so as to be sure of a drink despite Viaud's watchfulness, and drawing. He was utterly indifferent to current events. Sometimes, in a flash of tenderness, he drew the features of an employee of Renée Vert, the milliner from the Faubourg Montmartre who had married Adolphe Albert. There is a small picture of this girl in the Albi museum—an immensely charming one, showing an intelligent face, framed in a coil of tawny hair (page 251).

The theatre had lost much of its attraction for Lautrec, but at Natanson's request he designed a poster for Jean Richepin's *La Gitane* at the Théâtre Antoine. Marthe Mellot, Alfred Athis' wife, was acting in this piece. Her beauty and her voice had already charmed the painter three years earlier, when he made a drawing of her for the cover of No. IV of *L'Image*. As though wishing this to be his farewell to the theatre, he also did a portrait of Coolus; but he was not entirely pleased with this, and it had to be snatched from him to prevent him from painting it out. Was his hand losing its skill? Joyant took him on holiday to the Baie de Somme, and there he needed more than ten sittings to paint a portrait of his friend, dressed for duck-shooting in yellow oilskins (page 262).

This year, 1900, was decidedly inauspicious. Lautrec was a member of the jury for the Poster Section at the Exhibition, but he had to be taken round it in a bath-chair. The family kept him waiting for his

ENGLISHWOMAN AT THE STAR, LE HAVRE, 1899
Museum of Albi

allowance, and even tried to whittle it down; he went to Malromé himself to discuss this failure to fulfil their promises. Once there he calmed down a little, playing with the children, beginning a large portrait of Viaud in eighteenth-century admiral's uniform, and drawing every day.

Rather than spend the winter in Paris, he decided to settle at Bordeaux, where he found a flat for himself and Viaud at 66 rue de Caudéran and a studio in the rue de la Porte Dipeaux. There he set to work with a kind of frenzy, painting Cocyte, 'a fat whore', who was playing in *La Belle Hélène* at the *Grand Théâtre*. He also painted Mademoiselle Ganne, who had the title-role in *Messalina*, an opera by Isidore de Lara, and the old violinist, Danda. He was pleased with the *Messalina* and sent it to Joyant so as to raise some money; for now he was increasingly short of funds, a thing he could not bear, and though he had never before shown the slightest interest in what his pictures would fetch he now began to fuss about their prices and wanted to sell more and more.

A sudden stroke deprived him of the use of his legs. Thanks to his mother's skilful nursing, however, he made yet another escape from catastrophe. Was this a warning? Lautrec made no comment, but his sole desire was to get back to Paris and straighten things out in his studio. It is strange to find him, who had always been so negligent, suddenly bent on classifying his work and making out a kind of list of it, though he refused to believe it was finished. Electrical treatment had restored the use of his legs, and his brain was not at all affected; so he was handed back to Viaud and at the end of April 1901 the pair returned to the rue Frochot.

Lautrec's one thought was to resume work; but he seemed to have become the mere shadow of himself. He was thin, his gait was unsteady, and his hand slow as he toiled over portraits of André Rivoire, the poet, and Raquin, the architect. André Rivoire was the Secretary-General of the *Revue de Paris* and a great friend of Paul Leclercq, and he had written several articles on Lautrec in art magazines. He told Leclercq how the painter's hand began to shake after scarcely an hour's work, compelling him to break off; but all Leclercq could do was to inform Gabriel Tapié—who, alas, knew only too well what was wrong.

The young doctor had called on his cousin, who immediately suggested painting the famous sitting at the Faculty of Medicine, at which Tapié had defended his thesis two years previously. Lautrec duly painted this picture, which is so academic; sombre and impasted as to show no trace of his earlier verve and freedom of drawing, and prompted even himself to wonder 'Who am I?' Yet glory was his, assuming that glory is measured by the yardstick of prices! At the Depeaux sale, *Woman at her Toilet* fetched four thousand francs; *La Pierreuse* went for two thousand francs and *En meublé* for three thousand. Lautrec made a final selection among the pictures in his studio, signing some and throwing away others. It was a though he sensed that he would never come back there again.

On 15th July he left Paris, seen off at the station by all his friends. Renée Vert, in a pretty hat, embraced him warmly, while her husband was almost in tears. He was going to Taussat, relying on the sea air that had always set him up before; and there he stayed, in infinite weariness. About 15th August he was paralysed by another stroke, and Countess Adèle came to take him to Malromé.

He had to wait nearly a month for death, lying semi-conscious in bed, while the sun ripened the grapes on the estate and brought to a head the hatred of a world which could not forgive him for so lucidly describing its vanity and putrefaction. He died on 9th September 1901.

At the risk of seeming pedantic, one feels that the time has perhaps come to speak at greater length about Lautrec's medical condition, particularly in the light of a thesis published a few years ago at Albi by Dr Pierre Devoisins. Among earlier opinions, Dr Séjournet diagnoses achondroplasia of delayed onset; Professor Maurice Lamy, osteogenesis imperfecta, and Dr Gaston Levy, multiple epiphyseal dyplasia. All three agree that his condition was present long before the fractures which crippled him. Lautrec's height at the age of eighteen was five foot one inch, the minimum required for military service in France, and not the stature of a dwarf. The diagnosis

WOMAN AT HER TOILET: MME POUPOULE, 1899
Museum of Albi

IN A PRIVATE ROOM AT THE RAT MORT, 1899
The Courtauld Institute, London

therefore points to the conditions described by Lobstein, and by Porak and Durante, better known as osteogenesis imperfecta, but this condition would have been apparent at birth. Professor Maurice Lamy considered that the two fractures resulting, at an interval of a year, from what seemed to be very slight external causes, were examples of the spontaneous fractures of osteogenesis imperfecta. A further argument is seen in the fact that in typical cases these fractures are followed by a slowing down of growth and that this was found in Toulouse-Lautrec's illness. However, as Dr Devoisins remarks, 'it should be noted that Lautrec's growth was not merely retarded but completely arrested', and he goes on to present his own diagnosis, which runs counter to much that is customarily assumed, and thus deserves a prominent place in any biography of the subject.

Dr Devoisins asked Mary Tapié de Céleyran about Lautrec's visits to spas, and she confirmed the impression that they formed part of the ordinary holiday programme of the well-to-do, and were not prompted by any pre-existent pathological condition.

As for the fractures, the external causes were not so slight as has been assumed; on the first occasion a broomstick had been caught between the legs of a chair and on the second occasion there was a fall of five feet, which is enough to break even normal bones.

Having established these facts, Dr Devoisins considers other factors, such as the precocious puberty that Lautrec experienced. This inevitably stops the growth of the long bones, so that the trunk grows out of proportion to the limbs. Thus Devoisins has arrived at a diagnosis of adrenal disfunction which accounts for both the precocious puberty and bone deformities, and this is the signal achievement of his thesis.

Natanson has emphasized the effect of Lautrec's premature sexual development on his sensibilities. 'The slave of his exacerbated sensitivity and sensuality, he was by nature inclined to the unrestrained pursuit of subtle or exaggerated sensations. Every kind of perversion in love was more than interesting to him, it was a happiness.' He provoked them, arranged exhibitions of them, and Krafft-Ebing's study of psychopathology had become his bedside book.

One of the most important features of Dr Devoisins's thesis is the

242

emphasis he places on the value of first-hand accounts of Lautrec, though he shows them to have sometimes put friendship and decency before strict truthfulness, For instance, Joyant writes that 'It was a kind of paradox to see that a man who literally lived in brothels produced no erotic or sadistic work'; but Devoisins counters this by mentioning the lithographs made for Delteil, the mention 'licentious' which follows the titles of certain sketches in the general catalogue, and drawings in several private collections. As for the painter's alcoholic tendencies, Devoisins says he can find no family history of alcoholism, only the psychological cause. Toulouse-Lautrec was quite simply drowning his sorrows and making up for the emotional disappointments and physical defects revealed to him during adolescence. His artificial paradise of alcoholism was exceptional at first; afterwards the condition intensified, and towards the end of his life was more or less chronic.

Toulouse-Lautrec began drinking to excess about 1890, and the really disastrous period opened in 1898. Dr Devoisins sums up his condition: 'I have referred in earlier chapters to Lautrec's internment at Neuilly, his delirium tremens and the darkness that slowly descended over his mind and hand, and I will not revert to the subject except to quote what he himself said of his condition a few months before his death: "I am living on nux vomica, since I am debarred from Bacchus and Venus." '

To the ravages of drink were added those of syphilis. This he owed to Red Rosa, and no treatment then available could have completely cured him, even if he had followed one seriously instead of sporadically. General Paralysis was consequently the rapid outcome, the stroke from which he suffered in the summer of 1901 being one result of this. As Dr Devoisins says, Lautrec fortunately did not have time to experience the last stage of this General Paralysis, which ends in complete mental disintegration, for he died when still of sound mind, aware of himself and of those around him.

Other doctors have studied his case, and Dr Voivenel's conclusion that 'illness acts on genius, colours it and gives a particular cast to its production' is of help to us in deciphering the eternal enigma of

NUDE IN FRONT OF A MIRROR, 1897
Collection Mr and Mrs Ira Haupt, New York

artistic creation, which so often resembles the pelican's sacrifice, taken by Musset as a romantic symbol.

THE MOTORIST, 1896
Museum of Albi

SKATING PROFESSIONAL BEAUTY: MLLE LIANE DE LANCY AT THE PALAIS DE
GLACE, 1896
Museum of Albi

THE VISIONARY

'Lautrec's name stands for more than a body of work. It stands for a vision of things. It stands for a keenness of mind and of sensibility. It stands for a state of soul which penetrated the hearts of his contemporaries and has been perpetuated throughout our generation, partly owing to his technique, which was in itself superb, and partly through his extraordinary spiritual quality. Like all great visionaries, Lautrec was a precursor. He remains fundamental, like Baudelaire.'

E. SCHAUB- KOCH, *Psychananalyse d'un peintre moderne*

Anyone with a penchant for coincidences will find it curious that Lautrec's first big retrospective exhibition should have been held in June and July of 1914, to be cut short by France's declaration of war on 2nd August. The historians who assert that the twentieth century really began with that war and not with the year 1900 can draw a further argument from this; for Lautrec was the last great painter of nineteenth-century life, and the thirteen years between his death and this exhibition had to elapse before his greatness was established.

Immediately after his death there were signs of strong hostility. I will not linger over the insidious Lepelletier, an old friend of Verlaine

AT THE RACES, 1899
Museum of Albi

but a bad writer, who seized the opportunity for an outpouring of bile
in the *Echo de Paris,* not even bothering to get his facts straight: 'Like
the caricaturist André Gill, the caricaturist Henri de Toulouse-Lautrec
has just died in a nursing-home, after violent attacks of insanity, after a
terrible, vigorous struggle for healing and life .... Three years ago
already he had been shut up, but was afterwards able to emerge from
the horrible house of madmen ... Among the painters of his day he
will leave traces of his curious, bad talent, the talent of a deformed
creature who saw everything around him as ugly and exaggerated the
ugliness of life...' I will not pause over the articles in *Le Courrier*

THE MODISTE, 1900
Museum of Albi

Français and *Le Républicain de Lyon*, frequently quoted by Edouard Julien; but in any case few people came forward in Lautrec's defence. His family maintained unbroken silence. In 1907, after an exhibition had been held at Toulouse, Count Alphonse opposed a committee which wished to put up a statue to his son, and five years later he declared his intention of 'castigating' Gustave Coquiot, who was writing a book about the painter. The national museums were equally unforthcoming. Bonnat dissuaded the *Conseil supérieur des Musées*, of which he was the president, from admitting the *Portrait of M. Delaporte at the Jardin de Paris* to the Luxembourg, though it is a painting of exemplary restraint and sobriety. Not until 1914 did *Cha-U-Kao, the Female Clown* (page 197) gain admission to the Louvre as part of the Camondo bequest, while *Woman at her Toilet* entered the Luxembourg in the same year with the Pierre Goujon bequest. The only exception to this ostracism was the Bibliothèque Nationale, which as early as 1902 accepted Adèle de Toulouse-Lautrec's gift of her son's three hundred and seventy-one original lithographs, including early states, successive printings and complete sets.

The man who succeeded in reversing the trend was Maurice Joyant. He was undeviatingly loyal to Lautrec's memory, he had the support of Countess Adèle, and he never rested until he had published his great catalogue of Lautrec's work, persuaded the government to grant him the Palais de la Berbie at Albi as a Lautrec museum, and routed the foes of his adopted painter. All this had been successfully achieved by the time he died, twenty-nine years after his friend—in the same year as Countess Adèle, 'cousin' Tapié and Renée Vert. Everything done for Lautrec after 1901 was prompted by Joyant. It was he, in association with Francis Jourdain, who suggested and arranged the tributes paid at the Salon des Indépendants and at the Libre Esthétique show in Brussels in 1902, and—again with Jourdain—at the Salon d'Automne in 1904. Another militant propagandist for Lautrec was Arsène Alexandre, the art critic, who wrote the introduction for the catalogue of the Durand-Ruel exhibition of two hundred items in 1902, and for the show at the Manzi-Joyant Gallery in 1914. This, again, had two hundred items, including all Lautrec's finest works.

THE JOCKEY, 1899

Alexandre wrote that 'Lautrec was neither the warped individual whom some people affect to pity, nor the disorderly bohemian whom others delight in stripping of all his qualities and talents—in short, of all that made up his true self. He was first and foremost a man of delightful intelligence and great sensitivity, with a completely sincere outlook. The rest is merely incidental, sometimes superficial and amusing, more often painful beneath the surface, like everything that envelops or accompanies such rare, pure qualities as a man may possess.

'For those who could only judge by appearances, of course, Toulouse-Lautrec was a man of unfortunate physique, who often amused himself by using slang and who sought the material for his powerful compositions elsewhere than in the Faubourg Saint-Germain; it is true that in a spirit of bitter bravado and in his need for illusions, he sometimes resorted to stimulants of a too active nature. But when all this has been admitted and relegated to its due place, what remains of him? Everything . . . Not a stroke of his brush was meaningless or superfluous . . . The least touch of colour, the slightest pencil-stroke expressed, through much that was animal, much that was human.'

This, then, was where the painter stood on the eve of the world war, at the dawn of the new century he had foreshadowed as he recorded the old one by the quivering, opaline light of its gas-jets.

It is generally agreed that between the death of one cultural period and the birth of another there comes an intermediate period when standards are to some extent relaxed and morality descends from its pedestal—the moral code being at all times and in all places merely a system for defending the ruling caste, a body of taboos devised to maintain the status quo. And it is safe to say that between 1885 and 1900, when Lautrec was at work, and even up to 1914, the traditional nineteenth-century culture was degenerating and falling to pieces. Its literature was breaking up (the foundation of the *Revue Blanche* was extremely important, because it undermined the positions of the *Revue des Deux Mondes*, the bastion of Buloz, Flaubert, Ducamp and others); the rearguard of romanticism—Gautier, Baudelaire—was swept away. Another noteworthy symptom of this collapse was the appearance of a second-rate literary strain. Like the boulevard plays, the novels of Victor Joze, Marcel Prévost and other mediocrities, whose very names are now almost forgotten, had only a brief vogue. The secret trend was that of Marcel Proust, but it did not come to light until the war had broken out. The *Hydropathes* and Maurice Donnay's poems were alike in bearing witness to a new superficiality, to the substitution of mannerisms for ideas, feelings, and poetic rhythm.

In painting the break-up was even more patent. Here the great tradition of the nineteenth century had undoubtedly been romanticism, and it fought a rearguard action until the death of Manet in 1883. Impressionism reflected a determination to be bound no longer by what had hitherto been regarded as the visual norms. This explains the hostility of the reactionary middle classes, who kept away in a body from the Impressionist exhibitions of 1879, 1880, 1881, 1882 and 1887 or, when they did venture in, shared the indignation that led Albert Wolff to declare: 'They take a canvas, colours and brushes, place a few random touches, and sign the result.'

Hence there were inevitably two positions. One was that of a bourgeoisie clinging to its concepts of social organization (a dominant propertied class using the workers to produce goods reserved for its own consumption) and spiritual expression (the tradition of a style based on the study of antiquity, with noble themes, and academic standards of beauty to be defined by the Institut Français and by it alone).

The other position was that of the progressive bourgeoisie, who adopted the new outlook in order to retain control of the situation and, aware of the rapid development of historical materialism, made a virtue of necessity. This was the line taken by the Jewish bourgeoisie, by such men as the Natansons, Camondo and Blum (Léon Blum was a critic on the *Revue Blanche*).

The creators of a new spirit could look for understanding only to this latter category, and Lautrec is an outstanding illustration of the fact. His own social set rejected him, so far as possible, whereas the others accepted him because his way of looking at things did not upset them—they found it much less disturbing than Van Gogh's—and they had learnt not to shrink from facts.

ENGLISH SOLDIER SMOKING HIS PIPE, 1898
Museum of Albi

IN THE BOIS, 1897

Thirty years earlier, the bourgeoisie had trembled at the sight of Courbet's *Stone-breakers*, seeing their hammer as the symbol of a threatened conflict and the subject as too 'low' for beauty. But Toulouse-Lautrec's brothel women seemed no more hair-raising to contemporary bankers, rakes and real-estate owners than the odalisques in *The Turkish Bath* by Ingres.

The fifteen years of Lautrec's professional career were years of peace. The echo of colonial wars was as remote as that of the Paris Commune, about which the Goncourts spluttered so violently. History had to rely for its material on scandals, such as the Panama incident. The anarchist 'Terror' worried only the magistracy, who as usual were in the pay of the governing bourgeoisie, and felt their interests to be threatened. The one flare of real animation in the whole fifteen years was the Dreyfus case, which finally brought down the rickety structure of institutions inherited from Thiers. Economically, apart from increasing poverty—in which respect the 1914 war was singularly convenient for the bourgeoisie—inventions were promoting a new day of life; the telephone, electricity, the gramophone and even the cinema, the bicycle and the motor-car were all developing rapidly.

These fifteen years saw the emergence of a rationalistic man, believing in the virtues of science—a figure Anatole France shaped and polished as lovingly as he shaped his sentences—a man who had shaken off the trammels of religion. The fall of that last barrier delighted Lautrec, who found his mother's bigotry a burden.

Francis Jourdain emphasizes that Lautrec's talent was bound up with his period: 'Lautrec was a man of his time,' he writes, 'and this not only because he saw clearly the writhing features of his contemporaries. For all his show of indifference, not only to the development of society but even to that of the ideas which underlay it or were prompted by it, he could not live in complete detachment from that development, completely uninfluenced by those ideas; he could not avoid the effects of the mimesis which made him a very representative figure at the close of the nineteenth century. At what other period could an artist have been so free to consult his own whim and reject all constraint? At what other period could he not merely slake his thirst for independence but even feel it rise within him, conceive the possibility of a freedom that earlier custom would have completely precluded?'

Lautrec was of course a rationalist, and therefore escaped the anguish that afflicted Cézanne and Van Gogh (he found Van Gogh's philosophical and social mysticism prodigiously boring, but was too kind-hearted to tell him so). His work puts forward no demands, for he was not a pamphleteer, not a Léon Bloy or a Rictus; when he draws a prostitute taking some odious-looking customer upstairs he is not proffering an indictment of the bourgeois battening on a poor misguided girl—he just happens to have seen, on that particular day, a man with that particular face. Indeed, this truthfulness is really what some of his contemporaries found unpardonable!

Had he claimed to be lampooning society, he would have been regarded as a caricaturist, like Forain, and nobody would have cared what themes he chose; it was his air of saying 'I saw that!', in which he resembles Goya, that upset a section of the public.

To paint a man in the moment of sexual intercourse is to strip him down to his animal core; and this is Lautrec's strength as a visionary, for that core was soon to be laid bare by the great butchery of 1914. These women, many of whom were entirely bestial, would then show themselves in their true form, accepting the war, sometimes with sadistic joy, as a delivery from dependence on men, an excuse for pleasure. Anyone wishing for information about the mental state of the civilization in which Lautrec moved as a 'witness to the truth' need only turn to *La Vie Parisienne* or *Le Rire*.

Lautrec's work releases painting from all its current taboos, as Caravaggio had done in his day, and Courbet a generation before. He not only set up his easel in the brothel, lifting a corner of the veil that had so far concealed one section of society (which was in fact a secret society of pleasure, in contrast to the secret societies of the intellect, such as Freemasonry, so powerful between 1850 and 1900); he worked out a new technique of painting as well. Looking back from this distance, one sees that he could scarcely have adopted the impressionist technique! That lends itself admirably to sunny outdoor scenes. and particularly to views of nature in which the human figure is a

MESSALINA, 1900

Museum of Albi

mere accessory (Monet and Pissarro often use figures only to suggest form or colour as the top note in a general harmony; Renoir is an exception); but it is too delicate for an extremely penetrating analysis of attitude and character. It was because Degas saw things, and drew them, like a sculptor, that Lautrec cared about his opinion—and, be it noted, about nobody else's. It was because Jules Renard's style was compact, his descriptions both analytical and synthetic, that Lautrec enjoyed reading him. It will be remembered that when Lautrec visited Belgium and its art galleries, Cranach was the painter who made the strongest impression on him.

Lautrec never aims at prettiness or tenderness; what he wants is accuracy. The accusation of cruelty is unfounded in his case. He is not cruel, he is merely accurate. Louis Pascal was handsome, and remains so in his portrait. Oscar Wilde had flabby features, and his portrait shows them. Valadon's greed for gain, Red Rosa's bestiality, Renée Vert's sweetness, are all reproduced with absolute fidelity, and as art is nevertheless a form of interpretation, the painter displays this in his settings—the background of his portraits of Maxime Dethomas and of Monsieur Delaporte at the Jardin de Paris, or the impressionistic scene of Cha-U-Kao's dressing-room. *Woman in a fur*, painted in 1890, is almost hallucinating in the methodical precision of its treatment, the disciplined folds of the material, the texture of the fur, the modelling of the face. Lautrec never resorts to distortion except to convey movement, in his circus or dance-hall scenes; but his touch is disconcertingly sure, and that is why he was influenced neither by El Greco at one extreme nor by Vuillard, with his soft, spattering brush, at the other.

The extraordinary thing about Lautrec, or rather the thing that made him seem extraordinary to the public of his day, was that he alone, among all the painters of that period, set down exactly what he saw, without evasions, without comment and without distortion. In contrast to the erotic, suggestive art of the eighteenth and even nineteenth-century *petits maîtres*, to the prunes and prisms of the official Salon painters, who often verged on pornography (the *Belle Époque* was the age of suggestiveness, of whispering, of an eroticism at the

MAURICE JOYANT AT THE BAIE DE SOMME, 1900

Museum of Albi

AN EXAMINATION AT THE FACULTY OF MEDICINE, PARIS, 1901
Museum of Albi

penny-in-the-slot level of 'What the butler saw'), Lautrec shows life as he saw and experienced it. The reason why people found *Elles* so shocking was that in that album he describes women as a naturalist describes insects, women caught at any hour of the day and who are not posing, in other words not changing the slightest detail, the smallest facial expression.

Nothing is more terrible than truth; but whereas Zola, who also wished to show the truth, 'laid it on with a trowel'—to use an inelegant but accurate phrase—and the Théâtre Libre's productions overemphasized the madness, drunkenness and sensuality that were the keynotes of its plays, Lautrec describes what he sees as though drawing a horse and its harness. Francis Jourdain—I am always quoting him, but he is one of the very few who did not 'just miss' Lautrec, he understands him admirably—explains in his book that Lautrec was able to say what he wanted because he was able to do as he wanted. He did not believe that to give his life to art meant shutting himself up in an ivory tower. Dissipated he may have been, but never idle. Lautrec's life and his art were interdependent, they penetrated each other by a process of osmosis. He lived his art. For him, art was not a priesthood, it was rather the natural consequence of his inclinations. When he was lounging about in the Moulin Rouge, that is to say, looking at it, he was working. So he learnt as much there as when painting in his studio. One cannot imagine him leading a different life, or painting in a different way. There is no discrepancy between his life and his work, no pause in their synchronism, no hitch in their parallel development.

It is untrue to say that Lautrec's art is an instance of repression, that it was his misshapen body which impelled him to describe the seamy side of things, to open the 'doors of night' and cry to 'respectable' people 'Life stinks—can't you smell it?' Even the most shapely of men may be visited by an urge to shut himself up in a brothel, to sleep with prostitutes, to breathe in their atmosphere of vice, to get drunk, jeer at convention and cock a snook at polite society! The non-conformist attitude is not confined to those whose height is below average, whose looks fall short of Apollo's and who have never been loved by a woman. It is a natural characteristic, like kindness to animals or a bent towards a particular religion. Lautrec's was not solely a clinical case; pictorially speaking it gave proof of uncommon intelligence, lucidity and talent. It is a pity indeed to write of him in the language of a cheap novelette. His paintings, his drawings and his engravings, gathered in the wonderful museum at Albi and lovingly watched over by a curator with an unrivalled devotion to the work in his charge, are a pure, strong hymn to the truth.

LIST OF ILLUSTRATIONS

Numbers shown in italic type denote reproductions in colour

267

268

INDEX OF NAMES